A GOODNESS I CANNOT EXPLAIN

A Goodness I Cannot Explain

A Medical-Spiritual Memoir

Catherine Stewart

RESOURCE *Publications* • Eugene, Oregon

A GOODNESS I CANNOT EXPLAIN
A Medical-Spiritual Memoir

Resource Publications
An Imprint of Wipf and Stock Publishers
199 W. 8th Ave., Suite 3
Eugene, OR 97401

www.wipfandstock.com

ISBN 13: 978-1-4982-0919-9

Manufactured in the U.S.A.   10/21/2015

To those who face impossibly complex medical
and thus life decisions,
and to those who walk along beside them.

To the falling down getting up wild web of
those who make up what we call the church that follows Jesus,
because we need to hear each others' stories of grace.

Contents

NOTE TO READERS

Some readers will have picked up this book because they too have heard the words "We found something" or received a difficult medical diagnosis. Some who work in health care observe that many patients, upon receiving a difficult diagnosis, react in one of two ways: either "We will fight this" or "We are going to pray for a miracle." Many patients, understandably, find it hard to face and work with their fears. This book, recounting one person's story, offers an alternative to fight or miracle as they are typically understood. There is still fight in this story, and there is miracle, but not in the forms many might expect.

What is described here is no quick fix to the experience of fear and anxiety that accompanies a diagnosis. I do not want to raise false expectations about a simple way to make a decision and deal with fear. Nor do I want to make an assumption about a reader's experience and spiritual practice. What is described in this book is a path, a way of seeing, a way of paying attention. I cannot claim to predict how and where that path could lead a reader. Hopefully this story also offers both permission to feel fear and encouragement to seek after the wellspring of mercy I believe is there, holding together all that is, longing to reveal itself and be present to us, in both explicable and inexplicable, predictable and unpredictable ways.

Was it you?

Was it you
who asked me
"What would you need?"

Was it you
who pierced my malaise
broke through
to what I know?

If it was you
If it was your voice
If you knew what to ask
because you knew
what I'd know to answer
because you knew
what I'd need to know
to climb into the boat
and let myself be carried,

If it was you
then I will sit in this boat
and trust myself to the ride

darkness no matter
pain no mind
ignominy no threat

If it was you.

PROLOGUE

I MADE IT HOME through the snowstorm that night and went straight to the bedroom of my fifteen-year-old son. It was near midnight, but I knew he would not be asleep. He had heard the results of my evening in the emergency room: the CT scan had found something. I needed to assure him, "Don't worry, because the doctor says it isn't too serious."

A few days later, driving him home from school, I asked if he was worried. He replied, "No, because you told me not to be." I was stunned by the simplicity of his trust. So that's what it is like to be childlike, the virtue Jesus commends when he says, "Unless you change and become like children, you will never enter the kingdom of heaven."[1] You simply trust what your parent says!

If I had been able to see my son's face, maybe I would have recognized the obvious: the sullenness and anger. Now, on top of everything else that year, he had to deal with a mother's brain tumor. But I couldn't see his face and so created my own storyline. My agenda had taken over: in what would I trust, when the most prized part of my body had suddenly been thrown into jeopardy? It would be a labyrinthine journey, into fear and then out again, before I myself could enter the childlike trust that I now only imagined.

A few months later, I lay on a gurney outside Operating Room No. 8 in Sunnybrook Hospital, Toronto. Under the hospital gown, I was completely naked, for what was about to happen inside my skull included my belly as well. My surgeon appeared, reached into the chest pocket of his white lab coat, and, with a flourish, pulled out a pen. "See, I told you I would

---

1. Matt 18:3 (NRSV). All Biblical citations are from NRSV unless otherwise indicated.

remember," he teased. He wrote his initials on the lobe of my right ear. That was the deal we had agreed upon after I had boldly floated the possibility that all those very smart people in the operating room might just make a mistake. The initials were to assure me, before going into surgery, that they would get the correct side of my head.

I was rolled into the operating room, introduced to the team, and then given a little something to "help you relax." That is a euphemism for "anesthetize your body with some temporary poison for the next seven hours so you won't feel or remember while we shave your scalp, cut into your belly to get some fat to fill the hole we are going to make in your head, drill into your skull, destroy your ear bones, and core, scoop out, peel away, or otherwise remove what is pushing onto your brain."

And that is just what they did. A number of months later, a friend commented, "You must have been terrified on the day of surgery." Not until that moment did it strike me: I ought to have been terrified, given what was about to happen and all its possible morbidities. Novelist Ian McEwan gets it right when he has his neurosurgeon character explain, "Regularly penetrating the skull with some modest success is a relatively recent adventure."[2] I should have been afraid. But I was not.

How can I explain that? My lack of fear did not come by the avenue I expected. If you had asked me, pre-diagnosis, how a person gets through fear, I don't know what I would have said. If I were entirely honest, I would have said, "I have no idea." If I put on my preacher hat, maybe I would give the answer I thought the Bible taught: "We get through fear by trusting in God." And that answer still holds true, but in an entirely different way.

Over the years, in my work as a minister, I have talked with a lot of people facing fearful medical situations: stage IV invasive breast cancer, triple bypass surgery, multiple sclerosis, prostate cancer, approaching death. Some said they were not afraid because Jesus was with them. I wasn't sure I believed them. Others were frightened—and said so. I figured it was pretty normal to be afraid, and I was not going to lay some "Just have faith" burden upon those already feeling vulnerable. If fear could be taken away, that would be the work of the Holy Spirit. In my heart, I was skeptical that Jesus could take away fear for longer than a few moments.

The Bible tells many stories of people who are afraid. Angels appear to tell them, "Do not be afraid." Why not? Because God is good and God

2. McEwan, *Saturday*, 86.

can be trusted: "All things work together for good for those who love God."[3] When Jesus (even Jesus!) seems to experience fear in the Garden of Gethsemane at the prospect of impending death, his faith and trust enable him to enter death willingly. According to these stories, when God is given full horizon in our minds and hearts (when we totally surrender to the One who loves us), God's loving presence will displace human fear—of anything. With the story of Jesus' resurrection, early Christians entered martyrdom, apparently unafraid. But what do we do with such stories?

It is one thing to read in the Bible the nice idea that "perfect love casts out fear,"[4] but can those words help someone just diagnosed with cancer? It is one thing to sit in a church pew and hear the words of the apostle Paul: "We are afflicted in every way, but not crushed; perplexed, but not driven to despair; persecuted, but not forsaken; struck down, but not destroyed."[5] But it seems audacious to offer those words to a woman in her fifties with a line pouring chemo drugs into her veins in a last-ditch attempt to reverse the direction her body seems determined to take.

But somehow, somewhere back in the past, some people must have experienced something amazing that allowed them to affirm such audacious claims:

"Yea, though I walk through the valley of the shadow of death, I will fear no evil: for thou art with me."[6]

"The Lord is my light and my salvation; whom shall I fear? The Lord is the stronghold of my life; of whom shall I be afraid?"[7]

For the first forty-nine years of my life, I participated in these beautiful words without ever having to test them out with my own body. I had been in a hospital only three times: to deliver babies. My spirit and my flesh felt like a seamless whole; we ran together unencumbered. When the challenge of a brain tumor was put before me that day in February, I was afraid. If there were a way through the fear, I had no idea what it might be.

In my complete helplessness, I was led. I was led unwittingly. I only saw, months later, just how I was led: by a kind of prayer that I knew by the name of *Lectio Divina*, but which turned out to be far more comprehensive than I had imagined. I was led to an experience that broke through all my

3. Rom 8:28

4. 1 John 4:18

5. 2 Cor 4:8–9

6. Ps 23:4 (KJV)

7. Ps 27:1

learning and preconceptions about fear and God and myself and how human beings get through fear.

It came as a complete surprise when something actually took away my fear and that the way through the fear was not, at least on the surface, through any vision of or insight about God. It was about me. To my spiritual director, on the other hand, this made utter sense: knowing God is always intimately connected with knowing oneself. How did she know that? She is Roman Catholic, but I have also now found this wisdom in Protestant circles of faith. I don't know what prompted John Calvin to write, in the sixteenth century, "There is no deep knowing of God without a deep knowing of self and no deep knowing of self without a deep knowing of God."[8] Did he mean that only when we know ourselves as complete sinners, utterly depraved and dead to life, can we come to know God, out of our abject need to be saved? (That is a popular stereotype of Calvin.) Or did he mean that there is something deeply of God in all of us, that cannot be extinguished, and thus the journey to true self and the journey to God are inextricably connected? Or did he mean some version of both, held in a tight and loving paradox? Or did he mean something so entirely mysterious that it really can't be explained? Are we talking about the essence of the Christian gospel, that God loves human beings with a depth that is beyond our capacity to understand, but as we begin to receive and trust that love by faith, the positive regard we experience tells us who we really are and makes us, creates us? If this is what Calvin is talking about, presumably because he himself has perceived and experienced that love himself, then it suggests that the unexplainable can nevertheless be absorbed in some way, and thus affects how we live and the decisions we make.

My evangelical-Presbyterian childhood had drilled into me the first meaning: "The most important thing to know about yourself is that you are a sinner." Nothing in graduate level theological studies had been able to dislodge the notion that had sunk in very deep: God was God and I was Cathy. A chasm of sin and other assorted human traits and tendencies distinguished one from the other. How could I know God by knowing myself? But my experience with this tumor pushes me toward the latter interpretations of John Calvin's words: the possibility that as I pursue the path, practice the path of Cathy-in-God (turn to God in faith), I will discover the presence of God-in-Cathy. God dwells in Cathy, and the two cannot be

---

8. Calvin, *Institutes*, 15.

4

separated, even when she fails over and over again in love. The possibility those words hold is incredibly graceful.

Also incredible was the journey to that place of no fear. The people along the way—family members, friends, doctors, physiotherapists, and parishioners—matched and enforced the sense that my body was being held by a goodness far greater than I could imagine. I am tempted to say that all these circumstances, this goodness, were the miracle that I cannot explain. There is truth in this. Many people of faith would affirm the idea that coincidences are God's way of remaining anonymous.

But there is more. There is a deeper sense to "miracle."

At one point along that journey, my son asked incredulously, "Do you pray about everything?" A few years later, in the middle of a job interview, a retired accountant leaned forward in his chair, his eyes wide: "Do you mean you made a medical decision through a prayer practice?" The answer to both questions is yes, because I have been led to see that there is nothing, no matter how mundane, that is not within the purview of the Gentle Physician who seems to know me inside and out, flesh and bones included, as in the words of Psalm 139 (ISV), "You have examined me."

Maybe mine was an experience of God speaking through the flesh. Christian preachers talk about incarnation, usually at Christmas time. We mean God dwells in Jesus' flesh. But what about the promise that God comes to dwell in our bodies too?[9] What can that look like?

On the day of surgery, when I submitted myself to the drill and skill of a team of neurosurgeons, there was a kind of surreal aspect to it all. I say surreal because shouldn't there be some kind of pain that leads one to surgery? Some kind of disability? The tumor was pressing on my brain stem, and my cerebellum was misshapen, but I felt great. My cerebellum, that little computer at the base of the skull, with forty million nerve fibers connecting it to the cerebral cortex, more nerve cells than all the rest of the brain combined, more rapidly acting than any other part of the brain,[10] was firing away as usual.

I knew that the surgery itself would have a greater effect on my body then anything the tumor had done so far. To risk a list of possible disfigurements and impairments for what causes no pain? To let oneself be knocked unconscious in order to come out the other end with 50 percent chance of

9. John 17:21
10. Leiner and Leiner, "Treasure at the Bottom of the Brain."

having a normal face and who knows what other damage? That requires a lot of trust.

And I had been given the trust needed. Maybe therein lies the miracle. I became able to enter into a death because I had an experience of being known. This, for me, suggests a different meaning to miracle. Are miracles about the emergence of trust? Trust that God is more real even than death? We tend to think of religion in terms of belief and knowing something. What if it is rather about being known—and knowing we are known?

Matthew's gospel talks of the "pearl of great value"[11] for which a merchant sells all that he has. I had always thought of that pearl as something outside of myself (the kingdom of God) that I desired to attain by good and disciplined behavior. But what if we reverse the image: Jesus is the merchant and we are the pearls that Jesus seeks after in order to enjoy them? As we come to know ourselves as pearls, we also bestow pearls on each other, moving gracefully through the world. Somewhere along this medical journey, I began to feel as if someone was stringing a set of pearls to create a necklace and placing them, one by one, around my neck. The pearls were added slowly, as yet another person was good to me, yet another apparent coincidence opened a door for me. But the biggest, fattest pearl of all, sitting in the center, was something completely unexpected. I was the recipient of an extravagant goodness, which I could not possibly explain. A commonplace challenge to Christianity is "How can you believe in a good God who allows so much evil to occur?" But what about the goodness? What is to explain that?

What follows is not an explanation, but rather an account, of extravagant goodness that took away fear.

11. Matt 13:45–46

I

"We Found Something"

God be in my head, and in my understanding
God be in my eyes, and in my looking
God be in my mouth, and in my speaking
God be in my heart, and in my thinking
God be at my end, and at my departing, Amen.

SARUM PRIMER

Now that I look back, the tumor was probably making its presence felt long before it was detected. Six years earlier, I had gone to my doctor and described some odd dizzy sensations in my head. A blood test showed I was exceedingly low on iron, an obvious explanation for my symptoms. After a few months of iron supplements, the sensations went away. Maybe the sensations were caused by low iron, or maybe they were caused by a tumor pressing on my balance nerve, and my brain found a way to cope with the new thing growing. Our bodies are so good at adjusting.

In the spring of 2006, my husband, my son, and I moved into a house in the woods at the edge of town. This move had been a long time in coming.

For seventeen years we had lived in the city, close to both the university where my husband, Ted, taught and the church where I ministered. In that house of double red brick and solid oak trim, within walking distance of every amenity, we had raised our three children.

But over those seventeen years the family homes around us slowly but relentlessly converted to student rental accommodation, and we looked for a way out. Finally it came: a house on seven acres of wooded land, adjacent to another hundred that sat undisturbed with no road access. It felt as if we owned the full 107 acres of white and red pine, sassafras, white and red oak, beech, ash, tamarack, hawthorn, black cherry, walnut, butternut, bitternut hickory, white spruce, beech, cottonwood, and the invasive buckthorn. There were streams, rocks, deer trails, exposed escarpment, and innumerable hidden surprises in those woods. It was an unbelievable gift, just waiting for people like us who didn't mind the inconveniences of trucking in drinking water and tending a wood stove in the winter.

We moved in May, with a flurry of renovations to a sorely neglected house. Our eldest daughter, Sarah, was married in July, moving into an apartment downtown with her husband while completing her undergraduate degree. In September, our second daughter, Miriam, moved into residence in a neighboring town to begin her degree in music. Peter, in Grade Ten in high school, would have preferred staying in town to be closer to his friends but begrudgingly agreed to move with his parents. Not particularly enamored with the woods, he did occasionally admit to enjoying the path through the horse pasture that he crossed on the twenty-five-minute walk from the end of the bus line.

Part of the charm of this new home was that it took only twenty-five minutes by bicycle to get to work. Ted regularly rode his bike, until in October his front wheel hit a rock going down our driveway. He braked hard, flipped over his handle bars, and shattered his kidney. Though his kidney healed entirely, ten days in the hospital turned into a harrowing experience. We were thrown onto a steep learning curve of "how to survive hospital-land": the need to advocate for ourselves within a complex system, the politics of an ICU ward, the hallucinatory side effects of morphine. He had recuperated enough by November that I could head off on my long-anticipated trip to Rome to learn more about St. Benedict, the culminating event of a three-year program for women ministers hosted by a Benedictine monastery.

Upon my return, I began to feel twinges in the back right corner of my head. I wondered if they were the aftereffects of a cold. They were never painful, rarely lasted long, and were always different. I did not worry about them, although when they persisted into January I did start to wonder if they could be signs of an aneurysm, which scared me: didn't aneurysms usually bring instant death? Should I go to the doctor? I suspected they would not think much of such vague symptoms, and I was loath to present as a hypochondriac. I suppose this was a certain kind of pride: pride in my health, pride in the strength of my body, fear of looking foolish or just plain wrong.

Sometime in January, I had a second kind of strange sensation. Standing in the aisle in a drugstore, my feet felt like lead and pressure was building in my head. I didn't feel as if I would fall over, but neither did I care to try moving. I stood rooted in place, and the sensation passed. Aware of these vague pains in my head, I told Ted that if I ever fell over, he was to take me to the hospital immediately.

My congregation had long attracted university people. At one point I added up the number of postsecondary degrees among them. If you put a lot of weight in academic degrees, it was more than enough to intimidate. But faith calls for a different kind of knowing, inviting us all to become like children. For most of us, the learning curve of faith remains steep our whole lives.

The core group of this Presbyterian church had been born into evangelical households, and even though they had grown out of some of the stricter reins of that tradition, there remained tension in the congregation as to how to interpret the Bible. So we were doing a series called "The Living Word," using some comments from Scripture scholar Walter Brueggemann as our starting point: the Bible is meant to raise questions more than give answers. It is to push us into conversations about mysteries rather than close down discussions with certitudes. It requires of us participation, wrestling, a stance of humility.

The advantage of proximity to the university meant there were always people willing to stand up in front of a crowd and risk speech (preach). I could sit and receive. On the first Sunday in February, it was a graduate student.

> In creation there is not only glittering beauty, but also ashes; and this latter, creation's shadow side, its utter dependence upon its creator, *adds* to its perfection. For the human being, this means that part of our created goodness is the fact of our origin in *dust*.

This is perfection because God is glorified all the more when my self-made "I" falls away . . . God is glorified as Creator, in other words, when I believe my own weakness is my strength.

In other words, we must not refuse our own weakness, but instead choose to dwell in it. (italics mine)[1]

It was almost as if these words were preparing our congregation for what was to come within a few days: we would all be confronted with our "dustness" and asked to embrace it.

The following Sunday I preached about our weakness in relation to a God we cannot understand, a God whom we cannot fit into neat categories of our making. A teenager in the congregation was grieving the death of a friend. I shaped the prayers that day with her in mind, trying to acknowledge the utter emptiness in the wake of death.

> You O God, who hold our lives
> though we hardly know it
> You who hold our lives and our deaths
> Thank you for yesterday's day
> Thank you for today
> Thank you for what has been given
> Thank you for what is being given
> Thank you for what will be given
> Thank you for this moment
>   which is really all we have
> Thank you that what You give us is life
>   each moment of time
> Thank you for what is given in each moment
>   insufficient as it seems to be
>   incomplete
>   never enough
>   partial
>   falling down
>   trailing off
>   never finished
> Hold us, we pray
>   when things threaten to end for us
>   when different kinds of death enter
>   when weakness enters
>   and we don't know how to stand
> Hold us, we pray.

1. Justin Klassen, unpublished sermon.

That prayer, written to meet another's need, soon came back as words I very much needed myself. How often, I wonder, do the gifts we give to others become gift to ourselves? Sometimes, in reading an old sermon, I can't imagine thinking such thoughts all on my own. I have no memory of how they came to me. People quote back to me things I have said, and I have no recollection of the words or the process that led me to them. They come to me as fresh and new as if someone else had formed them. They come as from the sky. They come as from some deep well I did not dig. "We are interconnected in ways we do not know"; "What we do to another we do to ourselves": these sound like odd mystical ideas, but occasionally the veil opens and we see how it can be so.

Look at what preceded my diagnosis: two sermons on the theme of weakness. Was this one of God's ways of remaining anonymous? It did feel as if, before I even knew my need, the gift had already been given. The food that I would need, it was there, waiting for me. Maybe that food is there all the time, and we just don't see it. Maybe God is so effusively generous with the food that when we do actually see it, it feels miraculous. But maybe it is just the seeing that is the miracle.

The following day, when I walked in the woods, I actually had the cell phone in my pocket already dialed to Ted's phone number at work, so all I would have to do was press the green phone symbol. I felt that uneasy about myself.

Tuesday morning I was at my yoga class. Week by week we had been slowly moving our focus up the spine. The previous Tuesday, we had fixed our attention on our necks. Today, it was the egg-shaped space that filled our skulls. I placed all my imagination there.

That afternoon I had two appointments at the coffee shop with members of the congregation. As I stood at the counter for my second chai latte, the familiar sensation in my head came again, except this time stronger than ever before: it felt as if my whole head was aflame. As I opened my wallet to pay, my hands shook.

That was it. I decided, "I'm going to Emergency," a rare kind of resolution for one who tends to ponder languorously over the most inconsequential kinds of things: Which restaurant to go to? Which sweater to wear? I had never taken myself into Emergency before, and in real emergencies I tend to err on the side of stoicism and "Is this really necessary?" It took flames in my head to overcome my fear of overreaction. I would go to the hospital, but there was no rush; first I proceeded with the conversation as planned. After forty-five minutes, I realized I was no longer listening well. I told the parishioner I did not feel well and needed to either call my doctor or go to the hospital. After five minutes of waiting on hold with the family doctor's office, I hung up and went straight to the hospital. Ted met me there.

By now, of course, the symptoms had long passed, as I knew they would. I had to fight the feeling that I would be regarded as a hypochondriac. Ted sat with me a while, but a winter snowstorm was brewing and he was hosting a gathering of graduate students at the house that night. He needed to get home. Uncomfortable with the ambiguity of my symptoms, he cautiously ventured, "Maybe it's just menopause?"

"*No!*"

"How do you know?"

"Menopause isn't a catch-all for *everything.*"

My daughter came by for a while, and then for most of the evening I sat alone. The nurses perhaps suspected something I did not: it was not good for me to be alone at a time like this. But how did I know what awaited me? At eight p.m. things were slowing down. The storm outside was finally working in my favor: only the really sick were venturing out to Emergency.

It was only later that I realized that the emergency doctor was one of the pearls going around my neck: he was not one of the many residents in training, but rather the doctor in charge of training residents. Had he been a neophyte resident, would this story have proceeded as it did? He asked a series of questions. I could tell he was running through a checklist of the most likely possibilities: heart attack? stroke? diabetes? high blood pressure? It was none of these. More stress than usual lately? I knew where that question led. If I simply replied yes, that would be the end of the interview. But neither could I lie. So I answered, "Yes, but . . ."

He suggested that my symptoms might be impossible to diagnose at this point, and I would be referred back to my family doctor. But then for some reason, he lingered over this decision, and after a pause, during which I felt my fate hanging in the air, he continued, "Tell me again about these last few days." I began trying to describe again, ending with the detail "but today it was much worse."

He responded decisively. "That clinches it: timing. CT scan before you leave tonight." At least I would now know if there was anything to worry about.

At ten p.m. the empty halls echoed as I walked to the radiology department, very slowly because the painful pressure in the back corner of my head had resurged. When the scan was finished, they asked me to lie there a few more minutes. Though I did not know it, neurosurgeons across the city were looking at the picture of my brain, deliberating on whether they needed a different CT scan or an MRI. The CT technician simply told me, "They're trying to decide if it's worth a few more pictures." I prayed they would decide I was worth it, so when she came and said, "Nope! You're finished!," my heart sank.

At about eleven p.m., the doctor came into the emergency triage room, which by then was completely empty. He sat down beside me and said, kindly, "We found something." I was more relieved that there was a reason to justify my being there, that I was not simply imagining things, than scared about what they might have found. I felt no panic, maybe because he himself did not project fear. "It's a three-centimeter sheath tumor on the nerve that goes to your ear. It could be one of three different kinds," and he rattled them off.

"Wow! Out of the blue!" I exclaimed, and he replied, "Yeah, humbling, isn't it? It's humbling."

I was stunned. Since when is "humbling" the first word out of an ER doctor's mouth to describe the discovery of a tumor? The word "humility," for me, is completely connected with Jesus, his life choices, and his teachings. It is a central theme in Benedictine spirituality. To hear that word, under the hard glare of ER room lighting, from a stranger, was like being wrapped in a warm blanket to shelter me against the cold. It was a sudden infusion of home.

An MRI would show more detail. The hospital could schedule that within a few days, rather than the months it might take if my family doctor ordered it. There was another pearl: I had come to the hospital.

I called Ted: "They have found something." He was shocked, but I quickly added that the doctor had assured it was surely benign and probably not too hard to remove.

A friend visiting at the house that night immediately mentioned an old friend in Toronto who was now a neurosurgeon, radiating cancerous brain tumors with the Gamma Knife. I now know what that is: a device that administers radiation with precision comparable to surgery. Maybe this doctor friend could offer some assistance? But I was not ready to take that in.

Even with the emergency room order, I had to scrounge up some assertiveness to make sure the MRI actually got scheduled. It was set for late Thursday evening. Invited to bring along a CD to help fight claustrophobia, I chose Bach; sheer beauty was surely the strongest foe against any fear. The Bach came through, despite the noise of the machine. The challenge the next morning was to find out who, of three possible doctors, would read it and get back to me. By afternoon, I found myself in the neurosurgeon's office looking at my brain on his computer screen.

But first came the clinical check-up: smiling, walking toe to heel in a straight line, responding to visual and auditory stimuli. Nothing wrong with me! When he expressed some surprise that I could walk in a straight line, I was indignant. "Balance? You should see me in yoga class, standing on one foot with a leg and an arm in the air." At that point, I had no idea why any of the things he asked me to do were relevant. Now I do. He was checking for signs of impairment to my balance, facial movement, and hearing, all of which should have been affected by then. Five percent of people with an acoustic schwannoma have no symptoms. I was clearly one of them. It would be a shame to lose such hardy nerves.

The neurosurgeon noticed words written on the silver bracelet on my wrist. I had hardly taken it off since Sister Luke gave it to me in Rome. He read the words, caught himself, and shook his head. "Just curious," he said. The bracelet is inscribed *I am a woman touched by grace*. It was a comfort to be reminded, in the foreign land of a neurosurgery examination room, of my core identity. I was, and am still, a woman touched by grace.

I can't say that I have always known grace to be my core identity. Rather, it has been something to which I have slowly come to cling. The clinging started in earnest when, at age thirty-three, I accepted my first position in ordained ministry in a vibrant congregation, alongside an older colleague. The first year went fine, but one day in my second year I was shocked to recognize a gut sense that something was seriously not right in this family of God. I did not know it at the time, but I was caught in the web of broken trust that inevitably tightens its grip around a congregation suffering sexual abuse and harassment. I tried everything I could think of to address the issues I saw, but finally conceded this was a wall, and I had a headache. I quit banging my head and cried out like the psalmists do. From that moment, I began to learn what it means to live by grace: I could no longer pretend to be in charge of my life. At every turn, I was at the mercy of something much bigger than myself, which I chose to believe was good. Since then, it has been a long, slow, meandering journey, moving deeper and deeper, moving from one "oh!" to another to another: an endless opening up that has kept drawing me further and further into what feels like truer life.

The doctor led me into his office and I was thrown into the first of many brain anatomy lessons. He showed me the MRI and the three-centimeter acoustic neuroma, or, more accurately, a vestibular schwannoma growing on cranial nerve VIII, which runs from the brain stem to the ear. There were three possible ways to enter the skull to surgically remove such a tumor. The appropriate entry was determined by its size and location. Mine required the translabyrinthine entry.

As he continued to talk, it slowly registered what translabyrinthine would mean: the complete loss of the perfectly good hearing in my right ear, because the tiny bones that make for hearing would have to be destroyed simply to get inside the skull. Another possible entry would save my hearing, but it would require pushing aside the cerebellum (another part of the brain) and holding it back for the six or seven hours of the surgery, which carried the risk of hemorrhage or stroke.

I was thus introduced to the world of medical triage: weighing one set of risks against another. Between ear bones and stroke, it was obviously no contest. "You have two ears!" the neurosurgeon commented, as if the loss of one of them was no big deal.

Would I still be able to play violin in my Celtic band with only one ear? I knew a woman who lost all hearing in one ear all of a sudden in one single pop. The only explanation the doctors could give: it must have been a virus. What if a virus visited my remaining ear and I descended into utter soundlessness? One of my greatest fears is claustrophobia. To be trapped inside my head? A wave of panic began to rise within me, but panic was clearly not a welcome guest in this office.

The doctor launched into the statistics about other possible casualties of the surgery: 20 percent chance of damage to the facial nerve, because it runs right alongside the ear nerve. The facial nerve controls every facial movement and expression, but his chief concern was the mechanics of the eyelid. The regular opening and shutting of the eyelid lubricates the cornea, which needs continual watering. Although our ability to see is governed by no fewer than four different cranial nerves, if the eyelid does not close, they are all for naught. So if my eyelid would not shut, he described Plan B: take the nerve from the tongue and graft it up to the eye, in the hopes that it would take. My brain, obviously still healthy, was madly computing. Hmm

. . . if the tongue loses the nerve on one side, that's got to affect the way it can shape itself . . .

"And how would that affect my speech?" I asked.

"Oh, you'd be harder to understand." (I was aghast. Did this man know what a preacher does?)

The pace did not slacken; then there was the cosmetic issue of the smile. With cosmetic surgery, they could make my face look normal in resting position. Noting the caveat, I asked, "And when I would try to smile?"

"You'd look like Jean Chrétien." Jean Chrétien was the prime minister of Canada and had suffered Bell's palsy at an earlier point in his life. He had a significant droop to one side of his mouth, and it affected the way he spoke. Tears began to roll down my cheek as the implications of "damage to the facial nerve" began to sink in.

The neurosurgeon proposed surgery within the next two months, with a projected recovery time of about six weeks, if all went well. There would need to be time for the nerves to readjust, for balance nerves on the left side to compensate for the loss of the right-side nerve, for the facial nerve to repair itself. I should take some time to absorb this and call him back to schedule the surgery.

When I couldn't think of any more questions, he said, "You can find your way out."

I later experienced a more compassionate side of this doctor. He did return a phone call on a Saturday evening and patiently answered a list of questions. That day, however, the ability to communicate compassion was not his strong suit. Maybe, compared to some of the other kinds of news he has to break to patients, my problem was small potatoes. It wasn't cancer, after all. But that day, the implications of "brain tumor" did not feel small to me.

2

I Am Held

A blessing is an act—by speech or gesture—whereby one party transmits power for life to another party. This act of transmission, which occurs in a world of intense interpersonal relationships, is not explainable in any positivistic terms. . . . The priest does more than "wish" peace, but rather by utterance, generates, assures, and bestows it.

WALTER BRUEGGEMANN, *REVERBERATIONS OF FAITH*[1]

I be brave for you.

CLARA, AGE FOUR

THE FIRST THING I did when I got home was sit down at my computer to compose a message to my congregation. I could not see a way to keep this medical situation private. This journey was going to rope them in, like it or not.

1. Brueggemann, *Reverberations*, 18–19.

A preacher is one who describes what the life of faith looks like. But she also has to live it. I had preached that life is a gift, that we are not our own, that each day is a gift, and that our lives are not in our hands. I'd sometimes wondered whether what I preached so articulately was just a bunch of beautiful ideas. Were those fine ideas ever tested in my own life, would I be able to live their demands? Now was such a time.

Writing to my family across the country, I could more freely express my fear: *Loss of hearing in one ear is not the end of the world. A facial droop would be harder to take . . . I won't be the same!*

A third group that needed to know was my Benedictine women. These were the thirty women pastors who had converged on Our Lady of Grace Monastery in Indiana twice a year for the last three years, coming from Texas to Alaska to learn traditional spiritual practices. The trip to Rome had been the culmination, to learn the story of Benedict. The thirty of us conversed regularly through a web listserv and prayed for one another.

A curious happenstance, the same friend who had been at the house on the night of the initial diagnosis was due for supper this night as well. He wondered if I felt up to it. I had no guide for what to do the first evening one has been diagnosed with a brain tumor. I said he should still come, as long as he could handle some crying. I did cry. It was strange: life goes on, there are other things to talk about, other people's lives, ideas to discuss. At one point he turned to me and asked kindly, "What do you need?" It was a good question, a truly Benedictine question. Every session at the monastery had opened with Sister Luke asking, "Is there anything that you need?" That is the Benedictine specialty: hospitality. But sometimes we don't know what we need. That evening, I had no idea. At another point, he reiterated his offer to call his neurosurgeon friend in Toronto, who radiated brain tumors. Even though none of us knew whether that doctor would see me, or even if my tumor could be safely radiated, the possibility of any other option to the scenario presented to me that afternoon immediately lifted the weight of the diagnosis.

I have remained a stubborn holdout in what seems to be a pervasive cultural knee-jerk praise of any new technology. I can't help seeing the downsides. Are there not threats inherent in communicating virtually? Are we so enamored with the research capacity of the Internet that we don't see that human beings need more than information? But that first weekend, the ability to communicate quickly with a lot of people in a short time (brute volume) was a gift, and it continued to be a gift in the months that followed.

This was a journey for which I very much needed others. That first weekend became a feast of email messages, from family, congregational members, friends, and Benedictine women around North America. I was humbled to realize how glad I was to be connected to a virtual community.

Words feed me. Words lift me. Words teach me. Words reassure. Words offer wisdom. Words create images for me. Words create a world in my imagination. I needed words, and they came flowing in, like a torrential river. These email messages, which persisted throughout the next few months of research and decisions and then hospital stay, surrounded me with love. They assured me that there would still be a recognizable "me" even with a face transformation.

I am convinced that all these words played a significant part in my eventual recovery and healing. Friends passed on information; they recounted others' experiences of this surgery; they gave me insights. They acknowledged my fears. They confirmed for me that gifts do not only come through strength. They come through sharing weakness. I realized that this story was not just about me; it was about how a community could gather around one in its midst and hold her up.

Jane of the Benedictine gang told me the story of her brother who had this same tumor. There were maybe even some upsides: *He likes the fact that at night he can just lie on one side and there is no noise.* She validated my fear: *I've often thought that having a droop would be a very hard thing for me to accept.* An elder in the congregation who had gone through a divorce alerted me to the challenge of dealing with the public: *The next while will be difficult, as you will have to deal with all the different reactions of people. Some won't know what to say, some will be oversolicitous, and others may give overused "churchy" comments.* My youngest sister, in the midst of a difficult divorce proceeding, was nevertheless able to reassure me: *And in spite of anything, you will always be you.* There was comfort even in hearing others wrestling to take it all in. My mother wrote, *I could hardly take it in what you were telling me yesterday . . . I think I had thought, "Well, she'll have surgery and it will be fixed." I hadn't even contemplated that there would be losses.* One woman, a teacher, looked up the word "humbling" in the dictionary: *One of its meanings is "unpretending." I guess after a week like you've had, there's no pretending we know the ins and outs, the hows and whys of our bodies and our lives on this planet.* A young parishioner, doing a cross-country ski race, tried to "get a gleam" of what it must be like to receive this news. He decided that whenever he was struggling with some physical suffering in the race, he would think of me; maybe that would "give the gleam." I was completely moved by the energy people took to try to enter into my situation and come up with creative ways to support me. They reached for something to grasp onto, and in their grasping, they held me. Love is endlessly creative, and love heals.

But there is yet more to this community of compassion. Most of us will go through some kind of scary medical situation at some point in our lives, and if not medical, then something else scary. I began to see how sharing this journey might become a gift to others. Walking through mine could help people practice their own possible futures. Rowan Williams calls the church a web of giving and receiving gifts.[2] That gift-giving sprung up immediately, and I was not just the needy one. I was giver as well.

What a marvelous economy, this web of gifts. Contra what is still being taught at seminaries—"Ministers should not show weakness; people need you to be strong"—this economy works differently. People are strengthened in their own pain when they realize they are not alone. None of us need to be alone. I needed to hear that my community would still see me as me even if my face changed. They needed to hear that the person they knew could walk into new, scary territory and still sound like the person they knew.

On Saturday evening, there was a music event at the church. I noticed that people had different capacities for responding to me. One man came right up and gave me a hug. Others seemed to shy away. Two women sat themselves down in chairs on either side of me. There were no emotional dramatics, simply a coming alongside, a "being with." That is what I needed. When something on the inside changes (the inside of my skull is not what I thought it was!), it is comforting when something stays the same on the outside.

It is strange how something very difficult can hold such good as well. As I approached the first Sunday worship service of the congregation since my news had been sent out, I was very aware of how much this group of people, over the years, had taught me. I came to them neither as simply "Cathy the pastor" nor "Cathy the woman/mother/now patient." I came to them as "Cathy who has fed and been fed, nurtured and been nurtured, taught and been taught by this group of people for years."

Their stories had become part of me. I remembered particularly a thirty-year-old woman who suffered a number of years of fluctuating and

2. Williams, *Resurrection*, 43–44.

uncertain health. She described to me the freedom and grace of moving, after some struggle, from "Why me?" to "Why not me?" as she came to terms with the diagnosis of multiple sclerosis. I was aware that with my diagnosis, some people would be struggling with the question of fairness: "Why Cathy?" I didn't feel that question. My freedom from this sense of injustice seemed largely, if not completely, because of that one conversation with one woman. How can one conversation settle in so deeply? Isn't it amazing how one person's struggle and learning can be simply handed over to another, sheer gift?

As Sunday approached, I knew what I was up against. Only a few days earlier a neighboring minister had told me that his wife had already undergone one round of surgery on a brain tumor and was about to go through another because the cancer had reoccurred. I confess: upon hearing of surgery on her brain, something shifted within me and I placed her into a slightly different category than myself. I scanned my memory of her: had I noticed any odd behavior on her part? Any non sequiturs in my brief conversations with her? I tried to recall.

It is humbling (embarrassing) to remember my crude caricatures of a brain tumor patient. How little did I know about the brain! How little did I know about myself! How often that subtle shift occurs. We move people into a category labeled "other" for any number of reasons: a mental health diagnosis, a disclosure of something from their past. Some defense mechanism in us says, "Other! Beware!" and we shift a human being onto a lower plane than ourselves. Now I would face congregation members who were surely at least a little like myself: maybe I had already been moved into the category of "other." I wanted everyone, but especially the children, to see me up close, so they might know for themselves that "she seems like the same Cathy!" I did not want them to be scared.

An elder delivered an old sermon I pulled out of my filing cabinet, but I chose to do the children's story myself. I took the words with which I habitually sent people off at the end of the service—*Go in peace; Have courage; Hold on to what is good; Give thanks in all circumstances*—and told them some of the things for which I gave thanks even in these circumstances: the yoga class, the emergency doctor, the fact that I live in Canada. Among other things, I was thankful that this church was a place where people could cry. Even though I knew that some hate to cry in church, I wanted to keep giving that permission. Maybe I wanted the permission for myself.

Clara, age four, was one of the children in the congregation. Her words, "I be brave for you!," confirmed that this was a journey we could all embrace. It also became evident that this was going to be a two-way street: apparently I had made it sound like a grand adventure. And I was opening the door for people with their own struggles to share. One woman living with the challenge of bipolar illness reminded me of what she had learned: life is a gift. I thought of the story of Jean Vanier, founder of the L'Arche communities. He gave up a potential career in academia when he realized how much he needed to learn from mentally challenged adults. He insists that those we regard as weak have the greatest gifts to give.

In my family growing up, I don't think we were trained in how to speak of our emotions. We were a WASP family. It was a cultural, generational thing (not to blame my parents). It was therefore moving to receive this very straightforward message from my brother: *It hurts that you're going through this, Cathy. I don't know how else to put it into words, but it does. You may have a better understanding of grief and pain than I do, and you may be coping really well, but I wish you didn't have to. It makes me sad that you have to confront such scary and uncertain things, with such difficult choices. I'm glad you have others around you as you struggle with this.*

Another minister in the congregation saw the new twist on a blessing we had sung for years: *"God be in my head" will never sound quite the same!*

3

EQUIPOISE

Above all, trust in the slow work of God.
We are quite naturally impatient in everything
to reach the end without delay.
We would like to skip the intermediate stages.
We are impatient of being on the way to something
unknown, something new.
Give Our Lord the benefit of believing
that his hand is leading you,
and accept the anxiety of feeling yourself
in suspense and incomplete.

PIERRE TEILHARD DE CHARDIN[1]

EQUIPOISE: A MEDICAL SITUATION in which there is real uncertainty as to which treatment would be clinically preferable.

In my initial conversation with the neurosurgeon, radiation had been ruled out as a treatment option because of the size of my tumor.

---

1. de Chardin, "Patient Trust," 102–3.

However, I was entitled to a second opinion, and as a very fine one so swiftly plopped itself into my lap, I took it. The doctors forty miles down the road offered me the choice of either surgery or radiation.

It seems to be an assumption of our Western cultural ethos that choice is a good thing. I am not convinced. Choices abound, and it is viewed as our right to have choices. Medical situations always involve some; we can always refuse treatment altogether, after all. The world of medical choice is becoming more and more complex as technology is able to offer possibilities unimaginable to people in previous generations. Some of the choices seem cruel: how does one decide between the risks of cancer and the risks of chemotherapy? And how does one decide based on risks given in the form of statistics, averages, and percentages? I have not taken a course in statistics. I don't know how to interpret numbers.

Looking back, I sometimes wonder about the meaning of this number of weeks (the whole season of Lent) when I wrestled with medical options, because I ended up having surgery, in the end, ostensibly for the very reasons it was recommended in the first place: the tumor was big. It was even bigger than initially thought.

But the journey to get there: so many gifts it held! Through all the medical research that was required to make an informed decision about how to treat my tumor, I was led to a place I did not even know existed. I was led down, down, through layers of meaning, through the numbers and the statistics, through images and metaphors that gave flesh to the numbers, finally to a place that held it all. I was a different person because of the route I had taken, and I don't doubt that the surgery was a different surgery, and my head a different head, and the outcome a different outcome than if there had been no journey. While I was in it, the decision-making process was like wandering in a maze, or a desert, going in circles, lost, with no signposts. It was only later that I saw my route had been closer to a labyrinth: circling, yes, but each turn taking me closer and closer to a center that would hold me tight. The medical research was the first, entirely necessary, step in the journey.

Within five days of my initial diagnosis, I was sitting in the office of a neurosurgeon in Toronto who specialized in radiating brain tumors with the Gamma Knife. He too outlined the basic three options: do nothing, surgery, or radiation. He immediately ruled out the Gamma Knife (one big shot of high-dose radiation)—there had been too many complications arising with tumors my size being gamma-ed—but he did raise the possibility of fractionated treatment (spread out over a number of smaller doses). He picked up the phone, and we had an appointment with a doctor at Princess Margaret Hospital for a week later.

In the week between these two appointments, when I was on hold from a medical point of view, a friend who builds and paddles canoes sent me a message that closed, in almost an offhanded way, with these words: *I'm looking forward to seeing you at sassafras time. Hopefully, by then, you will have shot these rapids and will find yourself in smoother waters.*

These words brought tears to my eyes. It wasn't until a few days later that I stopped to ask why and thus stumbled upon an image that would carry immense healing power for me. Over the years, my spiritual director has taught me to pay attention to my tears. I would be talking away to her. She would be listening, and then all of a sudden my throat would catch or my eyes film over. She always noticed. If she didn't stop me right away, she would not forget to ask later, "What were those tears about?" Inevitably, stopping to pay attention to my tears was the key to unlocking my experience. Slowly, I have learned to ask the question myself: what were those tears about?

Why did the metaphor of shooting rapids bring on tears? I began to ponder. When I was five, my father became the director of a wilderness camp in Lake of the Woods. I spent every summer there until I was eighteen. I learned to love the canoe. For many, a first ride in a canoe is a harrowing experience. You are very close to the water and feel its power intimately. Balance is everything. If you place your weight too far to one side, the canoe tips, and into the water you go. If you get broadside to the waves on a windy day, over you go. But if you have a teacher to show you the way, the canoe becomes a finely tuned instrument, carrying you into worlds unimaginable. You can learn how to get in and out of a canoe, from a dock, and even from down in the water, without tipping. You need not be stuck if you capsize, even in the middle of the lake, because there is a technique to empty a canoe of water with no land in sight. You can learn how to cut through waves so you are not taking their force head on; you can learn how to get where you want to go even when the direction of the wind is pushing the canoe broadside. If you are fortunate enough to be going in the same direction as the wind, you can cobble together a sail with towels or tarps and whiz along. You can galumph for sheer delight: stand on the gunnels at one end and, with deep knee bends, propel yourself through the water until you lose your balance and fall in. In trained hands, a canoe can spin on a dime, weave in figure eights, side step, and turn 180 degrees in an instant simply by the angle of a deftly inserted paddle.

Now I had the clue about the tears: the metaphor for this tumor trek conjured from the world of canoeing brought together something very unfamiliar (someone opening up my skull) with something familiar (shooting a rapid). To call the surgery "shooting a rapid" shifted its meaning. Shooting rapids has a particularly beautiful context for me: green pine and spruce trees along the river bank silently standing guard, watching and waiting, and the solid Precambrian granite rock, one of the most solid geological formations in the world, holding the whole adventure in place.

I know (now) that cancer patients are encouraged to find hopeful and comforting images and dwell on them. I didn't even have to go looking. It was plunked in my lap. The word "rapid" connected with the whole geography of my childhood that has always grounded me: one island in Lake of the Woods. That island, mostly rocks and trees, which I came to know intimately by scrambling and exploring day in and day out, year in and year out, had become part of me. I can go back to that island fifty years later and find exactly the same rocks, sitting at the same angles, with the same striations of grey and pink, the same soft slopes that I knew as a child. That landscape holds me in place.

Other canoeists could now help build the power of the image. *I picture you going along a northern river, seeing more rocks, with the current picking up speed and the landscape starting to blur a bit. I really pray your ride will be only a Class II after all is said and done.*[2] One friend reminded me of a prayer I had sent her when she was waiting to hear test results about a lump in her breast: *Jesus be my canoe.* The image was now firmly planted in my imagination. Little did I know just how huge a pearl this image would become.

One week after meeting with the Toronto neurosurgeon, I was offered an alternative treatment. Walking into Pencer Brain Tumor Centre, I could hardly believe my eyes. Leaving "basic hospital Spartan" at the threshold, we were ushered into "business office lush." The posh carpets and upholstery

2. The difficulty of a canoeable rapid is classified on a standard scale. Class I is fast-moving water with no serious obstacles. Class II is moderate: rapids with regular waves; clear and open passages between rocks and ledges. Some maneuvering required. Class III is moderately difficult: contains waves, rocks, eddies; requires expertise in maneuvering and scouting. Class IV is difficult: long and powerful rapids and standing waves; souse holes and boiling eddies. Powerful and precise maneuvering required. Not navigable without a skirt to keep the water out of the canoe. I had done I, II, and III, but never IV.

spoke loud and clear: "If you have a brain tumor, you need extra special care." It was like entering a different world: patients walked down the halls with limps or shaved heads. A tour of the facility showed us the breakfast bar, library, and free Internet connection. I found out later that this had been the gift of a wealthy patient who had a brain tumor.

Ted and I had prepared a list of questions to ask the radiologist. The bottom line was that he could do radiation, but medically speaking it was equally as valid as surgery. He called it equipoise. If I were younger, they would absolutely advise surgery. If I were older, they would advise radiation. But I was fifty: right in the middle. We asked, "What would you do? What would you advise if you had a fifty-year-old wife?" He really didn't know. The big risks to radiation were the 1 percent malignancy possibility down the road and the 3 to 5 percent risk of swelling, which might require surgery.[3]

With this interview, I was launched into a time of discernment. I met with two elders to plan for the church in this time of uncertainty. I figured it might (should?) take me about a week to make the decision. Little did I know.

A few days later I had my second MRI, this time with a dye that would give more information about the tumor—how vascular it was (how many blood vessels attaching to it and running through it)—which would give an indication as to how difficult it might be to remove. It proved to be not overly attached, so that was hopeful. The MRI results were now on a compact disc in my possession. I called it "Cathy's head on a platter," but fortunately only I was able to call it up; I was luckier than John the Baptist.

I had only recently discovered the poems of Mary Oliver and was working my way through a volume she had written after her life partner died. In the poem "Heavy," she talks about grief as something that one can learn to carry. It can't be put down, but perhaps, like the heavy water jars that African women balance on their heads (my image, not hers), we can learn to carry grief. It takes practice.[4]

I was prompted to ask, if I think of these two paths as two different kinds of grief to bear, then which grief do I feel I'm being given the grace to bear, or can learn, by practice, to carry and embrace?

---

3. See Appendix B for a more complete summary of the two treatment options, including differences between Canadian and US care and risk assessment that I learned years later.

4. Oliver, *Thirst*, 53.

I was asking myself a very fine question, but I couldn't answer it. I wrote up the results of three weeks of medical research, listing the pros and cons of the surgery and the radiation options, and went to talk with my family physician. I could tell that she leaned toward the radiation, saying, "If it doesn't work, you could always do the surgery." Since then, I have learned more of the risks of radiation that would question that advice. Neurosurgeons know that radiation welds the tumor onto the nerve, so that if surgery becomes necessary, it is virtually impossible to remove all of the tumor. The surgeon working on a radiated nerve needs to choose between two different goals, both good: preserve the nerve or completely remove the tumor. It is usually not possible to do both. This was a piece of information not described in the medical literature I found.

I now see that medical research was the first stage of what was becoming my discernment process, though at the time I didn't know it was stage one. I thought this was the only stage. I was simply doing what had always been my default and is the standard Western form of decision-making, which uses the left brain's strengths: analyze, categorize, evaluate. I tried to weigh the pros and cons using my intellect and logical mind.

The results of my analysis are shown in Appendix B. Even though it is full of medical and physiological terms, it may be of interest to the lay person for how it outlines the complexity of medical decisions. How is one supposed to choose between the advantages and disadvantages of two such different treatments? Between the value of an ear and an eye? Between long-range possible effects and short-term known effects? How can one possibly weigh and sort all the various statistics? I learned that one cannot; yet the research needs to be done and assimilated nonetheless.

After organizing all the medical data, I translated the two options into what might be their impact for my life. Medical procedures are never just technical interventions. They carry personal meaning. I asked myself these questions: Do I mostly want it out because it is like an enemy invading me, or do I regard it as part of myself, which I can live with? Regarding the radiation: Do I feel comfortable having a dead tumor in my head? Can I bear the current symptoms over the long term (if the tumor does not shrink and continues to press on my brain)? Can I bear the waiting with radiation's uncertainties and risk factors for three to nine months: the tumor may swell; I may develop hydrocephalus? And then for the following two years I would have to wait to see whether the treatment would stop the growth or shrink the tumor. For the rest of my life I would live with the possibility: Would

I be part of the 1 percent to develop a malignancy? Regarding the surgery, I simply ignored the 0.5 (or was it 0.05?) percent chance of death on the operating table (standard risk of any long surgery?) and assumed I would survive that far. On to the bigger questions: How would I handle the definitive loss of hearing in one ear and the likelihood of a drooping face? What is easier/harder for me: a visible and functional wound to the face (eye, ear, mouth) or the invisible and soft symptoms of possible pain, the worry about what the golf ball in my head is up to? To put it another way: What is easier/harder, dealing with the loss and grief of known facial palsy or the uncertainty of not knowing, waiting, and wondering?

Now, as I look back to what I wrote at that stage in the process, I see that I am asking all the pertinent and necessary questions. My questions go beyond the mere statistics, trying to get at their meaning. But I was not able to answer them. They simply seemed a dense fog. I could not make my way. When I finally did make my way, it addressed these questions. Was the posing of the questions good and necessary even though I could not answer them?

Somewhere in here, when I was wrestling to understand the difference between these two options, I called the original Hamilton neurosurgeon. I had prepared a list of about ten questions to ask him, and he walked through them with me. I can't remember how I pulled it off, but somehow I managed to ask politely how many times he had done this particular surgery, and he obliged me with an answer: about 150 times. That sounded like a good number to me. He mentioned that he would be on holidays until the end of the month, so I could take my time in making this decision, but I should call him back at the beginning of April.

Ted and I were invited to supper by a couple in the congregation. The man recounted how he had made the decision between radiation and surgery for prostate cancer and then how he had decided which surgeon. Someone gave him the name of the nurse who did postsurgical rehabilitation with people after prostate surgery, and he contacted her and asked: "If you had prostate surgery, which surgeon would you go to?" She gave him only one name: the surgeon whose patients she never saw because they didn't have problems. This, I noted, was health care wisdom from the bottom up. This story lodged itself in my memory. Though I did not know it yet, later it would become one of the pearls around my neck.

As people around me learned about my options, they tried to imagine themselves into my shoes and decide what they would do. One friend felt attracted to the radiation option because it left room for miracles and mystery. With the surgery, once the nerve was cut, there was no room for the mysterious resilience of the human body. Wrestling with other people's wrestlings was both a gift and a burden. Sometimes it felt overwhelming to have to deal with their questions and feelings. Others thought of angles I hadn't, and I had to sift through them. This friend's idea of leaving room for a miracle was something I had not thought of, and it tugged at my own deep sense of hope. I always want to leave room for the unexpected.

She asked the poignant question, "Which way are you leaning?" I was stuck right in the middle: equipoise.

4

Writing by Heart

I will put my law within them, and I will write it on their hearts;
and I will be their God, and they shall be my people. . . .
They shall all know me, from the least of them to the greatest.

JEREMIAH 31:33–34

ONTHS AFTER SURGERY, I was back at the Benedictine monastery, describing this juncture in my medical story to Sister Meg Funk. "I did all the medical research."

She nodded knowingly. "And it didn't help you make the decision, did it?"

No, it did not. Shouldn't the rational mind be able to sort out the facts, weigh the risks, and make an informed judgment? Many decisions are made that way. But we are much more than our logical capacity. How fortunate I was to have someone to guide me further.

Earlier, a month after my diagnosis, my medical research mostly complete, I met with my spiritual director. I had gone as far as I could with the default method of logic in which our Western culture is so steeped. Sister Mary led me further. She asked about images. She asked about movements of my spirit; she asked about the spirit associated with each option. We were now moving into a different kind of knowing, a more right-brained kind of knowing, a kind of knowing that I had been coming to trust, ever so slowly, by learning a different way of praying. Prayer and medical decisions can connect in a most beautiful way, but again, not in a way I anticipated.

As a child and teenager, I had been taught that prayer was talking to God. I had noted the way the psalmists yelled and ranted and sobbed and moaned. I liked that. I felt immediate companionship with someone like Moses who seemed to be able to have it out with God: "Turn from your fierce wrath; change your mind and do not bring disaster on your people."[1]

I liked Jeremiah's freedom to vent and complain and let it all hang out with God.

> O Lord, you have enticed me,
> and I was enticed;
> you have overpowered me,
> and you have prevailed.
> I have become a laughingstock all day long;
> everyone mocks me.
>
> Cursed be the day on which I was born!
> The day when my mother bore me,
> let it not be blessed!
>
> Why did I come forth from the womb
> to see toil and sorrow,
> and spend my days in shame?[2]

However, I had never seen a living person actually pray like those Bible characters. Rather, I was taught to pray in an orderly and well-proportioned way, using the acronym ACTS: Adoration, Confession, Thanksgiving, and Supplication. Praying regularly in this way, all the bases were properly covered. There is undoubtedly great wisdom in this practice. Maybe it is similar to the Daily Temperature Reading recommended to keep marriage partners in communication. There are five questions to address each day. If a couple does it every day, transformation in the relationship is supposed to be immediately evident.

For most of my adult life I had tried to pray in an orderly way. Occasionally I let myself slide into moaning and ranting the way the psalmists

1. Exod 32:12
2. Jer 20:7, 14, 18

did. But when I was in my forties I was introduced to a different way of praying called Lectio Divina, which would (eventually) change my life.

A subtitle to this book could be *How Lectio Divina Saved Me*. How can that be? Lectio Divina is a very old form of prayer, mentioned by Jerome in the fourth century and firmly entrenched by the sixth when St. Benedict incorporated it into his monastic rule. For sixth-century monks, it provided a way to "munch" on the Scripture that was read out loud to them periodically through their day. They were to listen to a selection from the Bible, and then ruminate upon it throughout the day. The hope was that the life-giving word of God would slowly become a part of them, transforming them, in the same way that munching on food transforms our bodies: it makes us who we are.

When I was first introduced to the Lectio form of prayer, I was struck that it was more about listening than speaking. It was more about paying attention to one's own inner responses to the food, for inklings of transformation being invited, than about venting to some being. Although this form of prayer looks like just reading Scripture, which might seem impersonal, it is very personal, because the same words from the Bible can nudge people differently. Lectio Divina gives permission to take seriously my own inner reactions to a passage. I am allowed to pay attention to what happens in *me*. This created the first inkling that prayer might be about intimacy. Intimacy was not a word I heard much at all growing up, certainly not in any religious context.

An initial description of Lectio Divina does not necessarily reveal what it has to do with intimacy. It is often taught as a four-fold way to pray by the Latin words *Lectio, Meditatio, Oratio,* and *Contemplatio*. In Lectio one simply reads the text. In Meditatio one meditates, chews, ponders, and ruminates on the meaning and message of the text. Oratio means prayer: one responds to the word with one's own words or songs or sighs. Contemplatio is about silence, doing nothing, waiting and listening.

In many ways, Lectio resembles the three-part method I was taught to study the Bible as a teenager: (1) what does it say? (2) what does it mean? (3) what does it mean to me (what does it ask or require or move me to do)? These three questions get at three different ways we know: the facts, the meaning of the facts, and then the impact, dynamic power, and call of the facts on our own lives.

But there is a big difference. As Bible study, the text can stay in the head. Jesus healed a blind man; it means Jesus cares for people; we should also care for people. In this form of study, there seems to be a clear right answer to the questions. Listening to this same story in a Lectio way invites an affective response. Where were you in this story? With which character did you identify? What needs healing in you? How might Jesus be speaking to you? In this conversation, there is no clear right or wrong answer to the question, because only you can answer it. Such questions invite intimacy.

Sister Meg in Indiana showed me, post-surgery, how in trying to make a medical decision I had unwittingly done Lectio Divina.[3] The medical research was Lectio, the factual, drawing on my cognitive skill. The questions of meaning and metaphor were the Meditatio, drawing on intuition. But that was still not enough. I had prayed (Oratio), and then I had done nothing (Contemplatio). I had walked down, down, deeper and deeper, until a moment of being exquisitely, intimately known and held. My intuitive, groping path suggests that the four steps of Lectio are actually not steps. They are rather names for different ways a human being can experience. We have our logical, intellectual mind that sorts and analyses and categorizes. But we also have other senses: the intuitive, the ascetical (moral), and the spiritual (contemplative). Our Western culture trains us in this first sense (the logical) and highly rewards those who excel in it. These other three senses are less regarded, less trained, less prized.

Lectio Divina can thus become a way of developing a fuller humanity. It uncovers an undervalued way of being. And if prayer is really about encountering something much bigger than ourselves, then we need more than our intellect. My medical research was absolutely necessary, but now I needed to travel more deeply, drawing on my other senses, so much less practiced, recognized, and trusted. The journey beyond logic had begun.

Spiritual direction was crucial to leading me beyond the dizzying array of statistics provided by medical research. I don't know how, but Sister Mary and I got onto the question of the 1 percent. That 1 percent was the chance, down the road, fifteen years or twenty, that the radiation treatment could produce cancer in any tissue it had touched. The number one is a very small number. What was so scary about the number one, when there are ninety-nine on the other side of the probability? But that 1 percent scared me. If the chances to get an acoustic neuroma in the first place were one in a hundred thousand, then the meaning of the number one changes.

3. Sister Meg teaches Lectio in a slightly different way, using the rubric of *voices*. The text has four voices (literal, symbolic, moral-dynamic, and mystical) and these correspond with the four senses of a reader: logical, intuitive, ascetical (personal), and spiritual.

Mary asked, "Do you have an image for it? What does the one 1 percent look like?"

The 1 percent was a small, dark, cartoon-like figure, nattering constantly, clinging to my right hand, jumping up and down, and not letting go. In my mind, this figure represented death. Mary continued, "How does Christ treat the 1 percent? How does the 1 percent relate to the other 99 percent?" The scheduled reading for church that week was Luke 15, the parable of the lost sheep. Its words were fresh in my mind: "Which one of you, having a hundred sheep and losing one of them, does not leave the ninety-nine in the wilderness and go after the one that is lost until he finds it? When he has found it, he lays it on his shoulders and rejoices."[4]

The message seemed clear. Christ was saying to me, "If you end up as the one, in a deathly place, I will go and look for you and find you and hold you and bring you home and give you all you need, give you the extra care that the one needs, that the other ninety-nine don't need." If I ever became the one with cancer, Christ would fetch me and carry me with great tenderness.

My sense that Christ holds the deathly 1 percent is a rock-like truth to me. I have no doubt in it. This parable, so vivid, had clearly stuck onto me and worked its way into my heart. I knew, on some deep level, that Christ would not leave me on the hillside, alone. The story of Christ's own life had stuck onto me as well: how he walked toward his own death and received the pain of death with resolution. I had preached variations of "Christ holds us in death" many times. Nevertheless, experiencing it through a visual image was much more powerful. The truth of it penetrated into me more deeply. The 1 percent is death, and Jesus went out and got it and brought it in.

Sister Mary suggested I bring the one percent creature into the presence of Christ. The face of Christ that came to me was from an icon in mosaic tile on a postcard I had received. I brought the 1 percent death creature into the presence of Christ's face. Christ said nothing, but he gazed at the death creature in a matter-of-fact way. The death creature nattered on for a while, but in the presence of Christ's gaze it finally petered out and, silenced, hung limp on my hand.

Because the death creature was holding my hand and jumping about, my arm was jerked around with the creature's movements, but the rest of my body was not affected, and my eyes participated in Christ's gaze. I looked

4. Luke 15:4–5

at the 1 percent creature in the same way Christ looked at it. Alone with the 1 percent, I was overwhelmed. It took over my whole landscape. But when Christ came out to get me, lost on the hillside, or when I came into Christ's gaze, the death creature was seen for what it was: much smaller, a natterer that did not fill the whole horizon. Christ was simply much bigger and stronger and not fazed.

If the 1 percent represents death in the radiation option, is there a death creature or something that represents death in the surgery option? The death in the surgery is the 100 percent certainty of hearing loss (no probability factor there) and the 20 percent risk to the facial nerve. One hundred and twenty are bigger numbers than one, but less deadly. These deaths affect my vocation of listening and speaking.

Sister Mary pushed further. "What is the movement of each path? What is the spirit associated with each? It is the spirit with which you enter each decision that will sustain you." I didn't know how to answer, but I tried.

The spirit of radiation is one of mystery and gift already. One mystery: I noted that the same friend had been at our house both on the Tuesday evening of the CT scan and on the Friday evening when I returned from the initial visit with the neurosurgeon. If he hadn't been there both nights, would I have ended up with the consultations in Toronto with two more doctors? Would I have ended up with a radiation option at all? Maybe radiation was a gift. Another mystery: why had I not yet lost my hearing and balance already, if the tumor was so large? No one could explain that. What is the meaning of being among the 5 percent who have no symptoms? Why destroy something that is still good? I note that the radiation option hooks me with its narrative. What a great story!

Radiation involves waiting. How am I with waiting? I have been practicing waiting for years now, as a form of prayer, waiting in cashier lines, being patient, living with not knowing. But this felt different. It is also different from the nine months of waiting in pregnancy. Pregnancy I experienced as entirely joyful and without fear, because I had confidence in my body.

Sister Mary advised, "Let the decision emerge. Don't rush it."

She suggested that I take three days with each option. The number three did not matter as much as the intentional nature of the time. I was to invite Christ to lead me through those three days, entering as deeply as I could, starting with the lesser consequences and moving toward worst-case scenario. If I couldn't write the last chapter, I was not to try.

So I planned out the three days on the surgery option.

Day One: I would replicate loss of hearing by putting an earplug in my ear.

Day Two: I would add to the earplug by using an eye patch and imagining temporary facial nerve damage.

Day Three: I would add a further impairment, trying to imagine permanent facial droop.

5

Two Trying Weeks

For if we genuinely love him,
We wake up inside Christ's body,

Where all our body, all over,
every most hidden part of it,
is realized in joy as Him,
And he makes us utterly real.

And everything that is hurt, everything
that seemed to us dark, harsh, shameful,
maimed, ugly, irreparably
damaged, is in him transformed

and recognized as whole, lovely
radiant in his light.
We awaken as the Beloved
In every last part of our body.

SIMEON THE NEW THEOLOGIAN[1]

1. Bourgeault, *Wisdom Jesus*, 135–36.

O
N DAY ONE I met with three nurses from the congregation for breakfast, keeping the earplug in my ear. One asked about the risks of doing surgery after radiation. One spoke of the burden of being measured in the radiation option. They told me a little more clearly how radiation works to kill cells: both by scrambling DNA and by cutting off the blood supply. One spoke of a game she plays with patients to help them make decisions, about dignity: what most affects and contributes to their sense of dignity and what would be hard to give up? Another spoke of the many unexpected and surprising gifts I would surely receive on this journey. I realized these three women held a world of experience of which I knew almost nothing. I was like a baby, being asked to point at my preference. The three of them did not express a leaning either way, but compassion for the difficulty of the decision.

In the afternoon I went to my Celtic music group practice, in which I play lead violin, still with the plug in my ear. I initially sat in my regular spot, which put my plugged ear toward the group. After a few songs, I moved to the opposite side, with my normal ear toward the group. It was better but still frustrating. When people gave me quizzical looks, I explained what I was doing. Our musical director said, "Oh, take it out for this." I replied, "No, I have to know what this is like. This might be my life." The recorder player was amazed that I would go to such lengths to make a decision.

Playing in a music group was definitely different with one ear. With my plugged ear toward the group, my own instrument filled most of the airwaves. And even when I moved so my good ear was facing the group, I didn't feel that I could hear as well even out of my good ear. One good ear facing in the right direction was still not the same as two good ears. I couldn't take in the complex mixing and intertwining of sounds.

The morning of Day Two (a Sunday), I took a shower and tried to imagine my eye not being able to close. I yelled to Ted, "How do I shampoo my hair if my eye doesn't close?"

Determined to stick with my plan, I did the preservice music rehearsal with earplug in. But I cried through it—this might be the last time hearing this group with two good ears. I let my tears guide me and took the plug out.

In imagining not being able to close my eye, I became aware of what our bodies do unbidden. We close our eyes to block out the sun, or keep out soap, with no conscious decision.

I tried to imagine needing to water my eye every hour. My brother had told me about a colleague who had acoustic neuroma surgery—she had to water her eye every hour. That would mean I couldn't even go through a whole Sunday service without watering. I guess I would become adept at doing it quickly, like during a hymn.

Day Three was the day to imagine facial palsy, drool, thick speech, no smile. It was too hard to imagine my own face drooping, so I found a way to sidle up to it. I imagined having a face-to-face conversation with someone else whose face drooped, so that I would have to "look upon it." In my mind, I created drooping faces for Vic (a physician) and my friend Carol. I imagined sitting across a table from each of them in turn. In my scenario, they both communicated the same thing: there are more important things in life than facial palsy. They continued on with their life with dignity, and people around took their cue from them. As they were matter-of-fact about it, so were the people around them. Although these scenarios were only imagined, they were deeply revealing and helpful. Facial distortion is apparently one of the most difficult social barriers there is, but I knew of people who obviously have coped. My high school gym teacher had a deep purple birthmark covering much of her face, misshaping it. She was a great gym teacher and laughed heartily. We all must know someone like that. But then there were the other stories of people who suffer and struggle. The two people I chose to imagine both gave me the gift of courage and hope.

Three days were not enough to enter into the implications of surgery. The ear was enough loss for one day. To observe eye-closing was enough for another. After three days I still had barely entered the more mechanical possibilities of thick speech, drool, chewing issues. I imagined drool coming out of my mouth and falling onto my text as I preached and letting slip an unintended expletive into the microphone. And how would I form sounds correctly if I couldn't use both sides of my mouth? I pressed down on the right side of my tongue to immobilize it and tried to speak.

A friend called and recounted the sad experience of his mother-in-law who had this surgery twenty-five years earlier. "Enjoy your beauty," she still says to her grandchildren. Post-surgery she became more volatile and outspoken, which was maybe not a bad thing for a woman in a traditional Mennonite culture! I wondered if this kind of surgery should be regarded as a form of brain injury.

At supper, my sister, visiting for a few days, talked about her own brain injury from falling off a ladder. On the surface, it seemed that the injury was only physical—a blank spot in her vision—but the neurologist's questions in the months that followed included an array of other aspects. Did she feel easily overwhelmed? Was it harder to make decisions? Did crowds and large groups of people affect her? She did experience all that and was relieved that he recognized some of the softer effects of the nerve damage. Nerves in our heads are never just about mechanics, it seems.

Do these stories carry any spirit? How about: "Why enter the brain unless you have to?"

My sister also told the story of someone who got brain cancer that couldn't be contained. It was rather gruesome.

As the three days came to a close, nothing of strong impact had emerged, except I knew I didn't like having only one ear. I decided to take my journal to bed with me and spend some time reviewing the three days in an intentional way. Ted was already in bed. Lying on the bed was a publication from Louisville Seminary that he had received at work and brought home. He had never received it before and did not know why he had received it now. Procrastinating on the work I knew I needed to do, I paged through it. An article titled "Broken Beauty" stopped me cold. The opening words were a quote from Annie Dillard's *Pilgrim at Tinker Creek*.

> I am a frayed and nibbled survivor in a fallen world, and I am getting along. . . . I am not washed and beautiful, in control of a shining world in which everything fits, but instead am wandering awed about on a splintered wreck I've come to care for, whose gnawed trees breathe a delicate air, whose bloodied and scarred creatures are my dearest companions, and whose beauty beats and shines not *in* its imperfections but overwhelmingly in spite of them, under the wind-rent clouds, upstream and down.[2]

Dillard's words opened a shockingly powerful door onto the surgery option, one that I immediately recognized as true. This image of a scarred survivor connected with so many other themes in my life, past and present. Most powerfully, it connected with the image of myself from a few weeks earlier, as I lay in bed and could not sleep. I had felt utterly stripped naked and vulnerable, but somehow also liberated from falsehoods and pretensions. I felt free.

It also evoked the stories of the frayed and nibbled prophets Hosea, Jeremiah, and Ezekiel who are asked to carry in their bodies a sign of God's message. Hosea is asked to marry a prostitute. Jeremiah carries a wooden

2. Dillard, *Pilgrim at Tinker Creek*, 245.

yoke over his shoulders.[3] Ezekiel is asked to put some baggage on his back and dig through the city wall to show people the truth of their situation.[4] God makes them into signs. What if a palsied face is the hidden truth about us all as human beings, which I might bear in a physical way? We are all distorted in some way, and life yet goes on.

Unwittingly I had now entered into the second level of Lectio and the question of meaning. What does it mean to have a palsied face? What are the images and metaphors that become attached to it? A palsied face is never just a palsied face, a cold and bare fact. The meanings that attach themselves to it powerfully shape how one carries such a face. I found Dillard's words so evocative that I postponed my shift to the radiation option to allow myself a full twenty-four hours to simply absorb this vision.

In this lull before I ventured into the second three days, I went to a prayer meeting. A little tradition had been developing in the congregation: as various women had faced major surgeries, we had offered them a presurgery circle of prayer. This circle was now offered to me. A group of women gathered in a living room. I was invited to tell them how they might pray for me. I described the two options, concluding, "I can't quite imagine actually moving into either one of these options," and started to cry. People sat in silence and waited.

I told them both of the ninety-nine and the one, and the Annie Dillard, which seemed to show how there could be grace in either option. I asked them not only to pray but also to lay hands upon me. At the end I asked for someone to bless me with the words of St. Patrick's prayer:

> I arise today through a mighty strength, the invocation of the Trinity. . . . I arise today through the strength of heaven: Light of sun, Radiance of moon, Splendour of fire, Speed of lightning, Swiftness of wind, Depth of sea, Stability of earth, Firmness of rock. I arise today through God's strength to pilot me.

We sat in silence. How does one end such a time?

That evening I tried to write up my reflection after four days with the surgery option. I would have a disability, a scar, and a wound. I would be stripped naked, and my life would be different from what I had known, but I would come out of it as a child, in a sense, learning to walk again. It would be a kind of rebirth into a different life, a visibly wounded life with a

3. Jer 27
4. Ezek 12

different kind of dignity, an inner beauty as a frayed and nibbled survivor, a casting off of all previous images and maybe falsehoods. I would join a different group of people, the visibly wounded.

Does one choose woundedness? Christ did, but how? Only by grace, I'm sure my Catholic sisters would say.

As for geography, the surgery would be at the General Hospital, which was on Barton Street in the north end of the city. Earlier that year I had gone grocery shopping at Food Basics, next to the hospital that houses the trauma unit. I was taken aback at how visible in the bodies of the shoppers was their poverty: missing teeth, scars, scraggly hair. People who shop on Barton Street wear their poverty on their faces. If I did surgery, I would be lying, physically, amidst the visibly wounded of Hamilton. That is where I would belong. Radiation, in contrast, would be done at a posh place in the penthouse of a hospital named after a princess.

What was the spirit of surgery? My life as I once knew it would be over. The words of the apostle Paul came to mind. He lists all the advantages with which he was born, and then he exclaims, "I gave them all up for the joy of knowing Christ." That is my paraphrase of Philippians 3:8, which just happened to be the scheduled reading for that week.

Back home that evening, I sat looking at a full cup of chai tea sitting on the coffee table in the living room. I saw Ted's foot close by and thought how bad it would be if his foot moved and pushed the mug over. Two minutes later, my own foot pushed the mug over the side. It broke and tea went everywhere. My sister and I calmly picked up the pieces and wiped the floor. No one freaked. Life goes on, amidst brokenness.

As I sat across the table from my sister, I remembered her experience of finding herself pregnant and unmarried. She too was a frayed and nibbled survivor. And now there was the concussion. The brain injury meant she was not allowed to drive a car, so she has spent hours on the bus. But she is still very much alive and very much still the sister I have always known.

For every spirit pulling me one way, I got another spirit pulling in the other. Maybe there is enough not-beauty in the world that we really don't need to add to it if we don't have to. If and when there is the need, then maybe Dillard's words are necessary.

In the middle of the night I woke up to the sensation that my right ear was closing down on its own. I panicked. Ted panicked. I could not stay in bed. At four a.m. I went up to my desk. If my ear was closing off on its own, that changed the weighting of the options—the surgery would not hold the same loss. I would have to readjust my thoughts.

When I came back down to the bedroom later, I remembered this was a sensation I had experienced once before—wax can fill the ear canal and close it off. I wondered if it was just earwax, so I poured in some mineral oil to launch the treatment. Within a day or two my hunch was proved correct: the wax loosened, and I could hear normally again.

Next came the three days of considering the radiation scenario. This was harder to imagine. There wasn't much I could do tangibly. The only image that arose was one of me standing, alone, looking out from a window in our house, with pain in my head that no one else could see or touch. Radiation needs room to swell, but with limited space in the skull, what would it press against? The cerebellum that would affect my walking? I had read an account on the Internet like this. Then there was my brain stem. At the end of the radiation's three days, I lay awake most of the night searching for a spirit in the radiation option but was drawn back to Dillard, imagining those words taped around my hospital room, on my operating table, memorized and shared with all who visited me, almost a mantra, sustaining me. I had to keep trying to return to the radiation option to search for a spirit.

I was aware that if I chose surgery it would be hard for Ted, maybe even incomprehensible to him, and that he might not be able to support it, though he said he wanted to support whatever I chose.

Part of me just wanted to get the tumor out, to have all the cards on the table, to know where I stood and so be able to move on. Surgery would be a decisive and chosen *krisis* that revealed the truth: we are all frayed and nibbled. But what about my vocation that involved speaking and listening? Or did my real vocation involve revealing? Revealing the deeper sense of the truth about us as human beings? Or was it a kind of pride to think that it was for *me* to reveal the *real* truth?

I made a diagram of each option, moving from best- to worst-case outcomes. I noticed that the best case for radiation was truly amazing: facial nerve undamaged, hearing maintained at the same level, shrunken tumor; no swelling; no development of malignancy. It could be called nothing less than a miraculous outcome for a very bad situation. Moving across the spectrum to the worst case, though, it became malignancy and death. But all the statistics pointed to miracle as the most likely outcome. With surgery, there was no miracle. There was certain loss from the get-go. But there was very little chance of death.

The narrative of how I got to the Pencer Brain Tumor Centre, it seemed to me, was miracle. But the radiologist did not present radiation as miracle, in any way. Not even in clinical ways. It was still, in his mind, only equal with surgery as an option.

My imagining work complete, I looked forward to a different agenda. Saturday was chipping day. The previous fall we had cut down many of the invasive buckthorn trees on the property. Now that they had dried some, our woodsman friend was ready to help us feed them into a rented machine to make wood chips. I donned my work boots and gloves and went out to help. Because nothing had arisen in the radiation, and I was still attracted to the Dillard, I again tried on the surgery option. Calmness about my decision lasted a few hours. Then a panic arose: "No!" I couldn't bear it any longer. I felt repulsed by the idea of losing the hearing in my ear.

I simply could not seem to bring together the moving Dillard words and the cold reality of facial palsy. But then, I couldn't bring together tumor and me yet either. It was as if they repelled each other with the force of two like magnets. But maybe the nurse/elder was right: our minds truly can't take it in. It's a form of protection for what we have to do nonetheless.

Why would I turn my back on things that are good: my ear's hearing, my face, and the miracles so far? They are all good. Why destroy something good?

The vigorous work of throwing trees into a chipper strained my left elbow. This injury would prove to be another pearl, though I did not realize it at the time. I iced my elbow, and the pain seemed to subside completely.

As a new week began, a deadline loomed. The Hamilton surgeon would soon be returning from his holidays. I felt the need to do something, to take this thing by the horns. I wanted my ears tested. If I already had loss of hearing on the affected side, then it would shift the weighting of the pros and cons, since I wouldn't actually be giving up my hearing. Maybe it was already diminished. I called my family doctor and requested a hearing test. There was an opening that morning. The test showed both ears normal, with the right having only a slight decrease in the higher range, which was also normal. So the hearing test did not give me any weighting. We were back to equipoise.

Next strategy: get some people to ask me questions that I couldn't squirm out of, to help me clarify. I called a friend who met me at the coffee shop. He asked me, "Of all the possibilities, what do you fear most?" My response was immediate: "The 1 percent." That felt clear. I had a gut fear about the radiation. That would put me in the surgery camp. I reported this to Ted. He surprised me with an interpretation I could not have imagined: maybe I feared the radiation because I had already chosen it. Maybe I didn't fear the facial palsy because I hadn't chosen it. Part of me wanted to grasp on to this explanation. It would mean a decision had been made. Another part of me, though, recognized another very evident truth: Ted really did not want to see me in the surgery camp. If this seems convoluted, it is. The mind's ability to come up with possible interpretations is endless and exhausting. The maybes multiply like a swarm of locusts. For every maybe, there was a countering maybe, and then another. There seemed to be no escaping.

Another friend asked, "In each option, what would be your prayer?"

I began with the radiation. "That I wouldn't be the 1 percent," I said, starting to cry. "And that I wouldn't spend the rest of my life fearing becoming the 1 percent. That would be a kind of death in itself."

"And the surgery?"

"That I wouldn't end up speaking like Jean Chrétien." At this point he began to imitate Jean Chrétien, and we both started to laugh. This was not kind on our part, and surely anyone who has had Bell's palsy would be offended to hear this. But even this unkindness revealed something: whereas the radiation was a kind of death, the palsy was something that could be held more lightly. Jean Chrétien, regardless of what one made of his politics, did not let his face stop him from a public role. He evoked courage.

Ted was now getting impatient with this process. He ventured that maybe I needed him to push me to make a decision. I said no; rather, what I needed was leisurely conversation time to lay out everything I had experienced. We set aside two chunks of time on the weekend.

On the Friday afternoon of that last week of March, I gathered a blanket and some water and took Ted out to the one flat rock in the forest that I had discovered. It lay in a jungle of bush, at the bottom of a hill, with just enough room for two people to stretch out. I had often come here with a ground sheet or blanket to simply rest in the bosom of the forest, listening to the wind in the trees and gazing at the swaying branches far above me.

In my childhood summers on an island in Lake of the Woods, water, granite rock, and trees made up the entire landscape. A mother with five children can't possibly supervise them all, so as we got older we spent endless hours jumping from rock to rock along the shoreline and exploring the forest. One favorite spot was a sheer, almost vertical cliff about ten feet high. It was clearly visible from the water but for a person on land it was hidden from view by thick bushes. At midpoint in the rock face was an outcrop that shaped into a smooth, up-facing concave, like the palm of a hand. From the top of the cliff, you could only reach the rock hand by free fall. But I had found a safer way to reach it, by squeezing up and under some low-lying branches off to one side and then inching along a crack. I would make my way there and nestle, suspended in the middle of the cliff, precarious-looking to an observer, but safe in the granite. I imagined it was the hand of God, as Isaiah describes: "See, I have inscribed you on the palms of my hands; your walls are continually before me."[5]

Now this rock, in a different forest, held some of the same sense of safety. This was the first time I had showed this discovery to anyone. I asked Ted to listen with complete openness to each option, without interruption. I recounted all the details of the journey thus far. He listened attentively and commented only at the end. "One option feels like a sign; the other feels like a gift. Interesting." He found the thoroughness of my process impressive. He would not have entered into the process so methodically. He would have opted for the radiation immediately and run from surgery. There was no way to master this decision, he warned me. I found these comments insightful and helpful.

Regarding my question about how the radiation option can be both miracle and potentially the most deadly, he reminded me that life itself is a gift that contains within it the reality of death. Does that make it any less of a gift?

This reminded me of a scene in Wendell Berry's novel *A Place on Earth*. Margaret and her husband Mat anticipate that their son, Virgil, who is missing in action, may never return. Mat rebels against what seems to be the impending loss. Margaret holds his death and life as parts of an indivisible whole.

> "Virgil," she says, as if to remind or acknowledge what they are talking about. "From the day he was born I knew he would die. That was how I loved him, partly. I'd brought him into the world that would give him things to love, and take them away. You too, Mat. You knew it. I knew so well that he would die that, when he

---

5. Isa 49:16

did disappear from us the way he did, I was familiar with the pain. I'd had it in me all his life."

A tone of weeping has come into her voice, though not openly, and Mat does not yet move toward her. The weeping seems only the circumstance of what she is saying, not the result—an old weeping, well known, bearable by an endurance both inborn and long practiced. The dusk is thickening so that their eyes no longer clearly meet, though they still look toward each other.

"But I don't believe that when his death is subtracted from his life it leaves nothing. Do you, Mat?"

"No," he says. "I don't."

"What it leaves is his life. How could I turn away from it now any more than I could when he was a little child, and not love it and be glad of it, just because death is in it?"

Her words fall on him like water and like light. Suffering and clarified, he feels himself made fit for her by what she asks of him.[6]

Does the death-in-life make life any less of a gift? No. But is there still grief and fear? Yes. We did not try to draw a conclusion from this conversation. We had another time set aside on Saturday. Ted simply listened and observed, and it was good.

Returning to the house, I happened to mention to my son, Peter, that I was going to make an appointment for some physiotherapy on my right elbow. The pain in my left elbow from the chipping work had subsided, but it reminded me that I still had pain in my right elbow from a previous injury. The therapy on that elbow had come to an abrupt halt with Ted's shattered kidney. There was no reason I should not go back to complete that work. I had the time. Peter laughed at me, saying, "I don't go to a physiotherapist every time my elbows start hurting!" I ignored him, and another pearl was strung.

On Saturday morning I continued my hunt for questions. I had breakfast with my friend Carol. She asked me, "What kinds of resources do you feel you have, internally and community-wise, to deal with each challenge?" I do not remember her asking me this question. I only know she did because I found it recorded in my journal. It was a question that washed over me. I could not answer it. The word "resources" has always struck me as so impersonal. But I did remember her closing words: "What if you stopped trying to make the decision?" I was incredulous: if I didn't make the decision, who would? If I wasn't the one doing something, who

6. Berry, *Place on Earth*, 262.

would? It struck me as an impossible, ridiculous, and paradoxical suggestion that left me feeling baffled, exasperated, and helpless.

That afternoon Ted and I went on a three-hour walk. Throughout, we talked as if it was all but decided: radiation surely made the most sense. But in the middle of the night I woke up and couldn't fall asleep again with a panic: what would those rays be doing in my head?

6

April Fools!

The very circumstances of your life will show you the way.

RUSSIAN ORTHODOX MONK[1]

I T WAS NOW PALM Sunday afternoon (and also April Fools' Day). My
daughter was playing in the orchestra of a student production of the
opera *Suor Angelica* by Giacomo Puccini. Sitting in the audience, I
wasn't paying attention to the music. The endless Ping-Pong game persisted
in my head: back and forth, back and forth, surgery or radiation, surgery or
radiation? Then I remembered Carol's words and decided to stop trying to
make the decision. I reached up, captured the air-bound ball with my hand,
placed it on the table, and laid the paddle on top. What happened next
I cannot explain. Within seconds, a voice emerged, with just four words:
"What would you need?" I took the question to mean, "What would you
need to make it through each treatment?" I could answer that question.

---

1. This was the response of a Russian Orthodox monk who lived in the forests of
Finland, when asked by a layperson "what he has learned from his many years of prayer
and monastic life." It is recounted by Frank T. Griswold in "Listening with the Ear of the
Heart," a paper given for Trinity Institute, May 1998.

For surgery, four qualities came to mind: I would need determination, obstinacy, resilience, and persistence. Later I would reflect on the distinct aspects of those four words, but at that moment, there was only one thing that mattered: I had all those qualities. And for the radiation? I came up with two qualities: light-hearted (about the 1 percent) and optimistic. By light-hearted I meant the ability to be non-introspective about the 1 percent. I did not have those two qualities. I can be hopeful but not necessarily optimistic.

A decision had just been made, although I had done nothing. Rather, a truth had revealed itself to which I could give myself because I knew it was true. I had a sense of absolute clarity and no fear. I told no one. I needed to see if it would shift again as other attempts at the decision-making had.

I did not feel I had come up with the question the voice had posed. Rather, it arose in the silence created by the stopping of the ball. I took it to be Christ's voice. In my years of spiritual direction, Christ's voice often came in the form of gentle questions. I noticed that the voice asked essentially the same question Carol had asked the day before ("What resources would you need?") but in different words. It had been translated into language that allowed me to answer.[2]

Arriving home from the concert, there was a phone message from the friend of the Toronto neurosurgeon. The two of them had met that week. Did I want him to recount the conversation? He didn't want to influence a decision if I had already made one. I phoned him back and he filled in more details. He reported that the neurosurgeon had said something like, "It's not good for any human being to live with that kind of uncertainty for that long." I took it as referring to one of the negative aspects of the radiation option: the long waiting before one knows if the radiation has actually killed the tumor. But maybe the uncertainty he was referring to was this treatment decision itself; this limbo needed to come to an end. And the doctor also passed on a message: if I wanted to hand this decision back to the medical profession, he was willing to make the decision for me.

As soon as we got off the phone, it became clear that Ted and I had different interpretations of what the neurosurgeon had said. If I thought he was giving an argument against the radiation treatment (thus pro-surgery), then that bothered Ted. A verbal skirmish ensued with Sarah and Peter. Sarah objected to this doctor's audacity that he might know what was good

2. John Terpstra includes some of my story in his book *Skin Boat*. He was the one who, in conversation, recognized what had happened: "It was translated!"

for me. I could tell that neither of my children liked the thought of surgery. Fresh from the experience at the opera, it worried me that my family had such a unanimous and strong reaction against it.

After a day of sitting with the voice's words, I decided it was time to break the news of the decision to Ted, even though I didn't want to call it a "decision" yet, only a leaning. It was scary to call it a decision—there was finality to that. So I sent him an email describing the experience at the opera, and then left the house to see my spiritual director.

I described to Sister Mary the last few weeks. She asked me to dwell on the moment when the question arose in the opera. I closed my eyes. At first nothing came. Then I saw the resonance of the opera question with the question that Jesus so often asks in the gospels, "What do you need? or "What do you want?" Whereas the initial fruit of the voice at the opera had been a sense of peace, now, as the implications sank in, I was overwhelmed with gratitude. The voice had directed me to what I hadn't realized: I already had what I would need for this journey. It had been given long long ago.

Determination, obstinacy, persistence, and resilience: on first glance, these words perhaps appear synonymous. They each express a form of tenacity in the face of resistance, but each conveys a different body posture. Determination feels like a slow "head bent into the wind" movement forward, like a tank: it just keeps going no matter what is in its way. Obstinacy is the unbudging, staying in place, like Rosa Parks on the bus. Persistence is a repeated action, like the pecking of a woodpecker on a tree or the "she kept coming" insistence of the importunate widow described in Luke's gospel.[3] Resilience is the bouncing back after having been knocked down or pushed aside, as the Syrophoenician woman who retorts back to Jesus' attempted dismissal.[4]

If I would need persistence, it has been a quality of my character (for good or ill) since I was at least ten. I remembered an autograph book given to me on my tenth birthday. I wanted my father to write something in it. He put me off several times. When he finally sat down with pen in hand, he wrote, "To the most persistent ten-year-old I know." That same year, 1967, was Canada's centennial. To celebrate, school children were invited to test their fitness by doing timed running, sit-ups, and a bent-arm hang. I had set my eyes on the prize: the gold badge. I remember the timed run and the desire that coursed through my veins, driving my arms and legs to pump

3. Luke 18:1–8
4. Mark 7:24–30

pump pump, as fast as they could. I did win the gold, not, I don't think, for any kind of natural athletic prowess but because of sheer determination. And when I was thirty-three, I outlasted a very difficult ministry situation largely out of obstinacy: I couldn't see what to do, but neither was I going to give up and throw in the towel. I simply could not bear to see the congregation further demoralized. I stuck it out until there was a resolution. During that time, an elder came and told me everything wrong with my ministry. I was obviously to blame for the church's troubles. I sat under that cloud of criticism for months until I realized that he hadn't made a single "I" statement, only a series of blaming "you" statements. I went back to him and requested an "I" statement. He tried to put me off with "Are you still stewing about that?" but I did not cave, and our conversation opened up a grace and healing that neither of us anticipated. Persistence? Obstinacy? Determination? Resilience? I had these qualities in spades.

Sister Mary told me that what I described had all the characteristics of an authentic spiritual discernment process:

a. There was a true choice, in the sense that I could do either option.

b. There was grace present in each option.

c. She noted that I had used the words "truth" and "freedom" in my account. I was not even aware that I had used these words, but to her, they were a sign of God's Spirit at work. I imagine this is based on how the gospel of John holds these words tightly together: "The truth will make you free."[5]

d. There was an observable release of energy once the decision had been made.

e. It was only a slight and subtle shift of weighting that allowed for the decision to be made.

Whereas the last few weeks it had felt as if I was going round and round in circles, going nowhere, bouncing back and forth, in fact it was really more like a labyrinth. If surgery was the center where I needed to end up, I had come physically close to it (as one does in a labyrinth) repeatedly before being finally able to enter into it. Though I felt like I was going nowhere, I had been moving closer and closer to the center. As is true in walking a labyrinth, one doesn't see where this maze-feeling path will eventually end up. The restful center opens up as a surprise.

5. John 8:32

We talked a bit about the resistance I would meet and how to handle it. She warned me that it would be important to keep the Annie Dillard words close to my chest, as holy words. *There was no way to explain my decision in any rational way. It was not rational.* Neither did it feel particularly courageous. It was not courage that moved me. It would have required courage to do the radiation.

Given this advice, I should have been able to expect the reaction I got from my family. But I was not. When Ted called around six p.m., late for supper, I asked if he had received my email.

"Yes, and I don't like it."

My heart sank. I had not anticipated his resistance. I had not anticipated that I might have to deal with his fears or convince him or explain.

At a meeting of church elders that evening, I recounted that I had made a decision and that the new and unexpected bend in the road was family members who didn't like it. Tears rolled down my cheek, and Maggi the hospital social worker nodded knowingly. Oh! So this was not uncommon, for family members to resist a patient's decision. Families are on a different timeline, and as much as they want to be supportive, it is not their body, their brain, their ear, their face. Even though Ted had said he would support whatever decision I made, it was impossible for him to jettison his own fears, try as he might. He could not imagine any good future. Later that evening I recounted more of my experience to him. He was skeptical. I realized we were both very tender, that his words were hurting me, and that it would be better if we stopped talking. We did.

We had stumbled into another kind of suffering: the suffering of those who accompany, the suffering of those whose body it is not, the suffering of those who have no power to decide but whose lives are nevertheless intimately affected. Whereas I had the task of a decision and it was my body, those close to me had another challenge: to let me decide, in freedom, and to trust in my decision, even if it was not what they preferred. Theirs was the challenge to release control.

Given the medical information we had, the choice of surgery could be seen as a masochistic attraction to disfigurement, a daredevil challenge to the statistics. The stakes were high: facial mutilation. On the rational level it made no sense—how could facial disfigurement connect me rather isolate me? As much as the opera brought peace to my soul, allowing me to move forward, it created pain for others. They had not heard the voice that penetrated into their core. They simply had to trust. I had to trust the voice, and they had to trust me. We are all so connected in such a web.

I had arranged for a phone conversation that morning with the Toronto neurosurgeon. He began with a series of questions: When had I last gone to a restaurant? What had I chosen and why? Fish or chicken or beef? When I queried this line of questioning, he replied impatiently, "Just stay with me." His point became clear: we choose what to eat depending on what we like or what we feel like. Chicken is not better than salmon in any way; it all depends upon what we like. It was the same for radiation or surgery. Radiation was in no way empirically or obviously better.

The neurosurgeon had developed a sixth sense over the years about what people would choose. Having presented the treatment options to a patient, he often made a bet with his resident before later reentering their room to see what they had decided. With no smugness, he told me, "I'm rarely wrong." His sixth sense about me, based on our one interview, had been that I would choose surgery.

In my own roundabout way, I had confirmed his intuition. And isn't it interesting that though my spiritual director had called my decision "not rational" and "unexplainable," here was a neurosurgeon able to give me a way to communicate the irrationality.

But I knew Ted would not be satisfied. So I pursued further: "What about my husband, who was convinced that radiation was obviously, clearly, empirically better?"

"He's off base, and what he thinks is irrelevant. It's your body." The doctor described how sometimes he needed to separate the members of a couple to allow the patient to state clearly what he or she preferred. He himself had a horror of general anesthetic and so would choose radiation. But his wife would choose the surgery in an instant. People just have to find something to hang their hat on: horror of something is a pretty clear peg.

I was still not convinced. Given such small figures of risk for the radiation (1 percent malignancy and 3 to 5 percent swelling) and bigger figures of risk for the surgery (20 percent chance of facial nerve damage), I wanted to know, "Why is it still called equipoise?"

He replied, "It is not about statistics. Thinking about it statistically is a misleading concept. There is no objective thing about this. All those numbers and percentages are unimportant. Both options are excellent. There is no way one could say that, medically speaking, one is better than the other."

This neurosurgeon, without reference to the levels of knowing of Lectio Divina, was nevertheless confirming its truth: statistics and facts are of limited use in a decision like this. We move beyond the reach of science here. This is about personhood. I was impressed that a doctor so highly skilled in scientific ways of thinking was also highly comfortable with his intuition and able to help patients with very personal decisions.

When I reported all of this to Ted, he found it interesting and surprising. This conversation with a clearly very smart doctor was crucial to bridge the gap between my mystical experience at the opera and Ted's analytical mind. This conversation was more than that: what an incredible gift that a neurosurgeon could also help patients navigate the emotional traps of medical statistics!

Nevertheless, a pit of despair dogged us. Now it was time for friends to encourage him, and after two days (by then it was Maundy Thursday) Ted graciously managed the words, "I'll come round. I just need time." And to his complete credit, despite his fears, he never again questioned my choice, for which I will always be grateful.

Ted and I had an appointment with a counselor and the topic of conversation was obvious: the tension my decision had produced. Ted had simply not let himself imagine what would happen if I chose surgery, even though he wanted to be open to both options, even though he knew it was still a live option for me. Now that a decision was made, he had to move from his head knowledge (she might choose surgery) down into his heart.

Isn't it interesting how gifts are given. Ted's resistance to my decision made me work to find a bridge between us. I groped for a way to help him understand what had happened at the opera, how it had not felt like making a decision but rather seeing that something was true and being able to move with it simply because it was true. A metaphor began to take shape. "It's like . . ." (I grasped for the words) ". . . it's as if . . . it's as if a boat came along, and I could get into it." The more I thought of it, the more helpful the image became. Indeed, that was what it was: I had been given a boat I could climb into. Ted's resistance, Ted's need, had yielded a wonderful gift. A story came to mind from Irish poet-priest John O'Donohue. Bonus: Ted had been the one to originally recount it to me. The story was from an interview played on the Canadian national radio station. A Gypsy woman with a young family had leukemia. In his role as hospital chaplain, O'Donohue had been visiting her frequently. One day, when he arrived, she asked him to open the window wide. He recognized the cue: she was going to die soon. When he received the nod from the doctors that she had but a few hours left, he shared her death's imminence with her because he had promised to be straight and hold nothing back. She was frozen with fear. He saw what she needed: words. As he wove his words for her, she moved from "blue terror" to "sanctified tranquility and peace." "What is spoken at a death bed," he reflects, is akin to "a little raft of words that is given to the dying one to move across to the other shore." This gypsy woman took the raft and found herself ready to say good-bye to her family when they came to her bedside that day.

That is what had happened at the opera: I had been given a raft. I could climb onto it. I didn't know where it would take me, but I knew I could trust it; it was something onto which I could place my weight, even though it might carry me into death. The sense of the trustworthiness of the raft would be at least an even match for the terror into which it would carry me. It was impossible to explain, except that anyone who had ever stepped into a small boat knew what I was talking about. Ted knew. He had been in a canoe. A bridge had just been built.

This metaphor of surgery as canoe ride moved to yet deeper levels of meaning. Up until now, the comfort of the image lay in its familiarity. Canoe was home to me. Now the metaphor deepened: canoe ride came to mean "chosen act of trust." The power of the metaphor lay in its starting point, a bodily sensation. The smaller the boat, the more vivid the experience. Lowering your body into a canoe, you can feel your body's weight displacing the water. There is an initial instability: you can feel the water initially give way underneath you and then push back; you can feel the tension increase between the skin of the boat and the water. You can feel the water holding the canoe more tightly. I am sure there is a scientific explanation for this; all I know is there is a distinct physical feel to that tension. The water is pushing back, pushing up, and your body is held in that space that is created by the impermeability of the shell. The shell creates a safe place to sit upon the water. The water is very close; you can hear its movement as it swirls around, but you are held, up and dry. You are both very safe and very vulnerable.

On another level altogether, this idea of placing my body into something reminded me of a story my father told at camp to describe what faith is like.[6] A tightrope walker had a rope hung across the river just above

---

6. This is perhaps based on the life of Jean-Francois Gravelet, born in 1824, who crossed over the Niagara River above the falls many times, once carrying his manager piggyback.

Niagara Falls. He walked across the rope to the other side and back again. The gathering crowd cheered. Then he went across pushing a wheelbarrow. The crowd cheered louder. Then he crossed again, this time with a sack of potatoes in the wheelbarrow. The crowd went wild. Then he posed a question to them: "Do you think I could go across with a person in the wheelbarrow?" "Of course! You could do that!" they replied enthusiastically. "So, who would like to be the person?" The crowd fell silent. They talked an enthusiastic line, but they did not have faith in him. To have faith would mean placing one's body in the barrow, trusting one's life to this person. That's what it means to trust Jesus: place one's very body into his hands.

That is what my surgery decision felt like—it felt like climbing into that wheelbarrow and trusting that the one guiding it, steering it, would get me to the other side. It was not baseless or blind faith; I had done all the research, just as the crowd had watched the tightrope walker with their own eyes. But to watch and calculate and observe and weigh the possibilities is one thing. To get in: that was something altogether different.

I had to get into that wheelbarrow; I had to climb into a boat. All I could do was step in and sit. I had no paddle or rudder. I was not in control. I was not the captain. I didn't even know where I was going to end up. I just had to get in and trust myself to the current and the wind. It was a profound act of trust.

The early morning of Holy Saturday was filled with waves of fear about my face and my ear. Ted listened, held me, and, though it would have been an easy path for him to take at that point, did not suggest that the fear meant a wrong decision. Maybe he saw a possible escape route for his own fear, a chance to persuade me out of this path I had chosen. If he did, he did not breathe it to me. I figured these waves of fear could mean either that I had made a wrong decision or that fear was a normal part of either decision and I just had to ride it out. Was this not, after all, the day Jesus descended into hell? Could we not expect this to be a hellish day?

Somewhere in amongst the waves of fear, I wrote an Easter sermon. There is something terribly true about that, too, that Easter comes smack in the middle of fear. Maybe that is the only place it can truly arise.

7

THE GEOGRAPHY OF EASTER

Jesus said to her, "Mary!"
She turned and said to him in Hebrew, "Rabbouni!"

JOHN 20:16

THIS IS THE FULL text of the sermon I preached on Easter Sunday, April 8, 2007, based on the story of the resurrection told in the gospel of John 20: 1–18.

The Easter experience, for the first disciples, had a geography. They go back and forth to and from the tomb, running, running at different speeds, stopping, looking in, not going in, going in, stopping and then going in. Just for fun, or curiosity, let's sketch out the story in terms of the physical movement, and let's also pay attention to what the three different disciples see. For I notice that all three disciples have a different experience at the tomb; they experience the resurrection in three different ways.

Mary comes to the tomb, sees the stone, turns and runs to the disciples. She does not look in. She sees only the stone rolled away.

Simon Peter and John start running. (We're going to assume it is John; the gospel writer refrains from naming him). John runs faster, coming to the tomb first. He leans over to look in, seeing the linen wrappings. But he stops there. He does not go in.

Simon Peter arrives and a new geography is explored: he actually goes in, and he sees more. He sees the linen wrappings that John had seen, but he also sees another cloth, the one that had wrapped around Jesus' head.

Now there is a further movement: John goes in. The text simply says, "He saw and believed." It doesn't say what he saw; presumably it's the same wrappings that Peter saw. Nor does it say exactly what or how he believed, just that "he believed." They leave the tomb, and now the story turns to Mary. We presume she followed Peter and John (did she run too?) and now stands outside the tomb weeping. Now, for the first time, she too bends over to look inside. But she sees something different, something more. She sees two angels, and they speak. They don't say, as angels are supposed to always say, "Do not be afraid." Rather they ask a question, which is more like what Jesus typically does: "Why are you weeping?" Mary replies, "They have taken away my Lord, and I do not know where they have laid him." She then turns around (therefore getting a different sight line), and again there is something new: she sees someone she takes to be the gardener. This gardener/Jesus now asks not one but two questions: "Woman, why are you weeping?" and then "Whom are you looking for?" She answers. And then comes the pivotal moment in the story. Jesus speaks her name: "Mary!" And we are told she turns *again*. Was she not already turned toward him? What kind of turn was this? It was the turn of recognition, for now she recognizes him and says, "Rabbouni!" And thus we have the first experience of the resurrection: she concludes and tells the other disciples, "I have seen the Lord."

She has been carried through death to an experience of the livingness of Christ and to a personal experience of him, an experience where she knew herself to be known by name, and she knew who was speaking her name to her.

Notice the "in fits and starts" nature of the approach to this moment.

Mary to the tomb, then back.

John to the tomb, but not in.

Peter going in, leaving John outside.

John going in too.

Mary staying outside, finally looking in.

Then the encounter she has outside the tomb.

Notice the gradual opening up of what is *seen*. This is not so much fits and starts but a slow expansion. With each person, something is added to what is seen:

First it is the stone that is seen.

Then the wrappings.

Then an additional head wrapping.

Then two angels.

Then one supposed to be a gardener.

Then it is the Lord.

It is not the Lord immediately; it takes a series of other things being seen before *The Lord* is seen.

This is *not* an experience like Paul's on the road to Damascus, with a blinding light and a voice. Nor is it, as Paul (later) imagines in Philippians, every eye shall see and every knee shall bow. No, each one of the disciples initially sees different things, so they each have a different experience. We are not told what Peter experienced. We are told only that John believed. The account that receives the most attention is Mary's. This is interesting, for she is not the one writing. The account is not in the first-person; it is not John the storyteller's own experience we hear in detail, even though he came to believe at the tomb. It is Mary's story that gets the attention, maybe because Mary is the one to hear her name. Maybe that is the criterion of a true experience of the resurrection, that one somehow hears one's name spoken by the resurrected Christ?

According to John of the Cross and Teresa of Avila, we all live within the living God, but most of us don't know it. And so if there is any journeying in our life toward God, it is a journey not "toward God" but toward consciousness that we are already in God. It is the journey toward awareness. I am going to call that the journey toward being named. And I'm going to suggest that it is being named, somehow knowing that the resurrected Christ is speaking particularly to "us," that allows us to go through death into the resurrected life of Christ. It is a journey of being carried.

Sometimes it is a journey that we experience specifically at the end of our lives, as we approach death. So it was for Doris, a woman who died not long ago. At Doris's funeral, her daughter recounted how, on the last two nights before she died, Doris had a vivid experience of being taken for a ride by someone she didn't quite recognize, but to a place she felt she belonged. After her death, it seemed clear that these vivid experiences, initially dismissed as the dreams or even hallucinations of an old confused woman, were indeed the experience of being carried, lovingly and tenderly, into her death, so that she was not afraid or anxious but full of wonder and peace.

John O'Donohue speaks of his role as a spiritual guide with people who are dying. What they need is some kind of raft to carry them through their fear and allow them to enter into the land they don't want to go to. Sometimes there is precious little time to find that raft or construct that raft. Sometimes there is little material available, and he scrounges. His job is to help construct a raft that is able to carry them on this journey they need to make, through what look like waters that will only overwhelm. Maybe the raft is the words of Psalm 23 (KJV), "Yea, though I walk through the valley of the shadow of death, I will fear no evil." Or maybe it is words like Isaiah 43, "When you pass through the waters, I will be with you; and through the rivers, they shall not overwhelm you. Because you are precious in my sight, and honored, and I love you."

When I first heard this recounted to me, I didn't really understand what was meant by a raft, or constructing a raft. Now I do. And now I see that it is not only an experience for the end of one's life, at the actual moment of death. Such a raft can be needed and used any day of one's life, for any day one might be called to take a journey one had not planned. I myself have been taken on a journey during this season of Lent. The journey began with a CT scan, then an MRI, and a visit to a neurosurgeon. Two possible new journeys were outlined to me, for me to choose, both described to me in chillingly accurate statistics and percentages, all based, of course, upon the most up-to-date scientific evidence and research: with the surgery there is 0.5 percent chance of morbidity on the operating table, 20 percent chance of death to the facial nerve, 100 percent certainty of death to the vestibular/acoustic nerve. With the radiation there is 1 percent chance of malignancy developing within five to twenty years, 3 to 5 percent chance of hydrocephalous developing within three to nine months of treatment, and possible pressing on the brain stem.

To me, that meant that both options held death in some form or other. While the actual chance of immediate death to my body was small, other forms of death were inevitable. And somehow I had to come to terms with all the fears. What would happen to my face? Would I develop cancer down the road? Fears have such tremendous power to gnaw away at our lives. I realized (though only once it was given did I recognize the experience): I need a boat! I need an experience of the living Christ carrying me through this! We all know, somewhere inside us, that every day holds the possibility of death; we know we could be hit by a bus, as the sixty-eight-year-old woman on Main Street East was hit this past week. We know we could have a vehicle accident or bike accident that lands us in the intensive care unit, our life saved by liters of blood someone has kindly donated. Or our appendix could burst, and all of a sudden our life is on the line. Or we could get a diagnosis about something growing within our breast, or our colon, or our lung. But we tend not to think about all that, most days. Most of us don't have the chances outlined so well to us, in statistics and percentages. Do you know what percentage chance you have of making it through the day alive? Or living through to the end of this year? We all take some form of that raft journey in our daily living, as we deal with fears, as we step into unknown territories, as we grieve losses, as we lose people close to us or things we've never known how to live without. Maybe all of a sudden (pop!) our ear stops working, or a leg, or a hand, or an eye. Or we go to Uganda or El Salvador or Haiti and see forms of death all around, or we work in a hospital and see death daily. Our lives are full of little forms of death, threats to our own lives and to others. And we need an experience of the livingness of Christ to carry us through these deaths.

So when the time comes, and we are confronted with the real possibility of some form of death in life as we have known it, and fear and grief arise, as they did for the three disciples John and Peter and Mary, we will find ourselves looking for some kind of raft to climb onto, to carry us through, to carry us through our fears and into that unknown land we cannot possibly imagine. If it is anything like the experience of the disciples, it might be a journey of fits and starts, or turning around and around in circles. It might be a journey that only gradually opens up into more and more, as theirs did. It will not be the same for any of us. But hopefully it will be a journey in which we know ourselves to be named, by One who knows us, and we will recognize the One who speaks our name, and we will be able to get into that boat, and let ourselves be carried by the One who has been there already, and carried many people: into death and through it, into the waiting presence of the living God who is, and can be, nothing but Love.

8

BARTIMAEUS MODE

As [Jesus] and his disciples and a large crowd were leaving Jericho, Bartimaeus son of Timaeus, a blind beggar, was sitting by the roadside. When he heard that it was Jesus of Nazareth, he began to shout out and say, "Jesus, Son of David, have mercy on me!" Many sternly ordered him to be quiet, but he cried out even more loudly, "Son of David, have mercy on me!" Jesus stood still and said, "Call him here." And they called the blind man, saying to him, "Take heart; get up, he is calling you." So throwing off his cloak, he sprang up and came to Jesus. Then Jesus said to him, "What do you want me to do for you?" The blind man said to him, "My teacher, let me see again." Jesus said to him, "Go; your faith has made you well." Immediately he regained his sight and followed him on the way.

MARK 10:46–52

I T WAS A FRIDAY night, about ten years earlier. A group from the congregation sat in a circle at a Sisters of St. Joseph retreat house. The leader read the story of Bartimaeus and invited us to pay attention: "Which word or phrase jumps out at you?" I knew immediately which words had caught my attention: "even more loudly." Bartimaeus was incredibly bold, determined, and courageous to persist all alone in the face of opposition.

64

He was doing the opposite of what I had been taught as a child: "Don't be selfish." He was clamoring about his own needs, his own body. Surely there were many others that day who needed or deserved Jesus' attention more than him. How could he be so audacious? And yet Jesus honored his persistent clamoring. Jesus called it faith! Bartimaeus's desire to be well and to ask to be well: that was good!

Going around the circle, we were invited to simply say the word or phrase that had jumped out at us. As we went around the circle, no one else had chosen, or rather, been chosen by "even more loudly." I was the only one. I was embarrassed. I must be wrong. There must be nothing special about those words after all. Why did they strike no one else? It soon became painfully obvious: these words had jumped out at me because they were exactly what I needed. I had long ago opened the door to a crowd of naysayers in my head, and they were a thriving gang. I needed Bartimaeus's words. I needed to learn to ignore the crowd. I needed to find my own voice and speak it boldly. I needed to learn something about the difference between loving myself and being selfish, as John O'Donohue teaches, "You can never love another person unless you are equally involved in the beautiful but difficult spiritual work of learning to love yourself."[1] Now, some years later, blind Bartimaeus was my needed companion. My healing would come despite the crowd.

Resilience and persistence: they were among the four qualities I had named in answer to the question at the opera. I knew I would need them to recover from the surgery. I had not anticipated I would also need them pre-surgery. But I did. I had needed resilience to bear the unexpected burden of those accompanying me. Now, with the medical system, I needed persistence because I wanted to give my facial nerve a fighting chance against all those menacing statistics. I now moved into Bartimaeus mode: fighting, clamoring, and yelling.

The Monday morning after Easter I took stock of the situation. I knew that the risk to the facial nerve depended largely upon the experience of the surgeon. The medical research described the risk as a matter of sheer numbers: how many times had the surgeon done this particular surgery? The Hamilton neurosurgeon had done about 150. Toronto, forty miles down the road, was a much bigger city than Hamilton. Surely that meant there should be surgeons with more of these surgeries under their belt. I had read in my research of surgeons in the United States who only did this surgery,

1. O'Donohue, *Anam Cara*, 26.

as often as once a week. They claimed a record of no facial nerve damage for tumors under three centimeters. This kind of experience would greatly boost the chances of saving my facial nerve and my vocation, I figured. I wrote to the neurosurgeon in Toronto, asking if there was anyone in the city who did this surgery with the frequency as some doctors in the States.

I guess the reference to American doctors was like waving a red flag in front of a bull. He was skeptical of the claims of the American doctors. It was hype to draw customers. No doctor in the United States would be better than the good ones in Canada. That was reassuring, but his advice, *Don't drive yourself crazy looking for the* 100 *percent perfect situation*, felt like an attempt to shut me down. This resistance forced me to clarify my motive. Whereas my natural tendency might be to just accept what was offered, I felt I owed it to myself (to my face and my vocation of public speaking) to at least inquire whether this was the best I could reasonably expect. The idea that I might rightfully clamor on behalf of my vocation felt absolutely novel to me. I replied back to him, asking for a name of one of his colleagues.

That evening I had a long phone conversation with my sister-in-law Elaine, who possessed an intuitive ability to enter into my experience. Why had I not called her earlier? She coached me: "*No one* can possibly know what they would do in your situation unless they are in it themselves. *No one* should even *dare* to say what they would do, or tell you what to do, because they are not in it themselves. What people think they know, and what they will experience when and if they do, are two completely different things. I know this from the experience of when my mother died."

She added one more quality to my list of what I would need: humility. It would take humility to live with a disfigured face given the weight our culture puts on appearance. We know that life is deeper than our faces, but it takes humility to live in it.

Regarding the 1 percent chance of getting cancer, she noted something I had not thought of: the impact of fear can be disfiguring, from the inside out, making it possibly *more* disfiguring than any outer change. This made her one of the first people to really acknowledge the power of that 1 percent to me. Others had said, "What's 1 percent?" She, though, pictured it as a hungry raven, sitting at the edge of our line of sight, but ever present, predating, and waiting for a way in.

She also impressed on me the importance to journal about this for the sake of others. "All you've done is climb into the boat! And what a rich story it is already. You are heading on a journey and dragging a whole busload of us behind you."

When I got off the phone I realized how much I needed such conversations. I was so close to the brink of despair. I needed to be pulled back, by something, or someone, each day. Elaine's ability to see why I had chosen surgery, and to affirm it, was strengthening. A number of people had told me they would have chosen radiation, or were afraid of the surgery. It did not seem fair that on top of my own fears, I needed to deal with other people's. I guess that is the nature of community, though. If we are connected at all, we are connected by both our strengths and our fears. We seep into each other's lives. People feared partly because they loved me; I needed to bear them too. But the ones able to walk alongside without fear, what a gift they were.

In her poem "When I Am Among the Trees," Mary Oliver talks about the saving power of trees. That poem became my mantra. I had memorized it, reciting it as I wandered in the woods:

> When I am among the trees,
> especially the willows and the honey locust,
> equally the beech, the oaks and the pines,
> they give off such hints of gladness.
> I would almost say that they save me, and daily.
>
> I am so distant from the hope of myself,
> in which I have goodness, and discernment,
> and never hurry through the world
>   but walk slowly, and bow often.
>
> Around me the trees stir in their leaves
> and call out, "Stay awhile."
> The light flows from their branches.
>
> And they call again, "It's simple," they say,
> "and you too have come
> into the world to do this, to go easy, to be filled
> with light, and to shine."[2]

That evening after the conversation with Elaine, I played with Oliver's words as I wrote in my journal. Some days it was the trees in my forest that saved me, held me, bore me. That day, it was my sister-in-law, and her

---

2. Oliver, *Thirst*, 4.

words. I wrote: "When I am with Elaine, I would almost say that she saves me. I am so distant from the hope of myself."

The next morning I received an email from the Toronto neurosurgeon: he had checked with one of his colleagues who works with my kind of tumor (non-malignant) and he gave even less promising percentages: 100 percent likelihood of temporary facial weakness and about 30 percent chance of permanent weakness. He advised me to stick with my Hamilton doctor.

With this information about Toronto neurosurgeons, I phoned the Hamilton neurosurgeon's office to give him the go-ahead to book the surgery. A recorded message greeted me: only in emergencies should one leave a message. That gave me an out. This was not an emergency.

Later I called back and got a real person: no out this time. Even given the opera experience, it was hard to spit out the words: "I am ready to book the surgery." The nice woman on the other end replied, "Vestibular schwannoma? That would be at the General, then. OK. I'll make the arrangements."

The support that pulled me back from the brink that day came from a group of church elders who gathered to pray for me. Maggi the elder had decided that she wanted to host a group once a week for the next while. Three were present that evening. I described once again the process of discernment that had led to the choice of surgery, and then I spewed out my list of needs: my waves of fear, my family's fears; the need for verbal messages and images; the need for a coach; hope for resilient nerves; the needs of the congregation; my parents; the surgeon and team; the use of my time presurgery; thanksgiving for the discernment given.

One of the elders present was an elder with whom I related with difficulty. We stood diametrically opposed on just about every social and theological issue. But he was the one who offered the prayer of thanksgiving for my discernment, and I could tell from his prayer that he got it. He caught the difference between a decision and a discernment led by the Spirit. He could affirm that it had been a spiritual process. This was good, probably for both of us: a bridge was built that was rooted in our shared and common ground. It was also humbling: people are complex. We too easily put them in boxes. There were so many unexpected gifts along this journey, just as had been predicted.

Back in Holy Week, I had gone to see the physiotherapist about my left elbow. As she worked on my elbow, I told her the decision for my head. She then told me about a colleague in Toronto who saw people like me post-surgery. Would I like to speak with him? If I had not, a few weeks earlier, heard my parishioner's story about his prostate cancer treatment, I doubt I would have responded. Why would I need to talk with a physiotherapist presurgery? They deal with postsurgical issues. But I recognized the parallel between the prostate treatment and mine (health care from the bottom up), and so I took the contact information, even though I didn't know what I would ask. After some email tag, I finally had a phone conversation with him. I don't remember much of the conversation. I think he told me some of the weaknesses I could expect. I don't even know why I asked, because I had accepted that the surgery would be done in Hamilton, but I asked anyway, "If you had an acoustic neuroma, is there a doctor in Toronto you would go to?" He gave the name of a doctor at Sunnybrook: "Dr. Bob has done a thousand of these surgeries." That was the information I was looking for. Then, without any further questions on my part, he added, "I would kick myself if I didn't at least explore the possibility of surgery with Dr. Bob." It was as firm a push as I could imagine.

This information threw me into turmoil. Would my family doctor refer me? Would my Hamilton doctor have already gone ahead and begun the process of scheduling me in Hamilton? Would Dr. Bob even see me? How soon? Would he take me on? Would I meet any criteria he might have for taking on a patient? Was Hamilton out of the catchment area? Would it mean a significant delay in treatment? I did not sleep well that night.

If this was my turmoil for that day, this email message from a woman in the congregation became the consolation: *During the last part of March, as I tried to decide what I would do in your shoes, I was totally convinced that radiation was the choice I would make (realizing that in the end I did not have to make any such choice). I know only too well what it is like to lose one's hearing in one ear and, well, it just made sense. On Palm Sunday (yes, April 1) I felt a total sense of dis-ease with that thought. As I was ripping apart the palms that morning, I felt that my conviction that this was the right choice for you was being ripped apart, but I could not explain this, nor did I say anything about it. That feeling persisted, and when you told the clutter of clergy on Good Friday of your choice, well, you could have pushed me over with a flick of a palm branch! And yet, I knew that it was right.*

Another person walking along beside me could intuit what I needed, against all logic. It made me feel not alone. And look at the timing. Who can explain that?

At an earlier juncture in my life, when I was dealing with an intense conflict in the congregation over a period of months, I realized I could relax with all the surprising and endless punches if I thought of them as the ups and downs of an undulating landscape, or the troughs and crests of a rough ocean. For every difficult, deflating moment that carried me down, away from the sun, away from sight of land, there would be an up that brought me back into light, back where I could see a wider horizon. I could roll with the downs more easily if I could expect an up to match it. Maybe that is what Paul the apostle meant when he wrote of the Lord saying, "My grace is sufficient."[3] Is it always so? Is there always a grace to match even the deepest descents? All I know is: the gifts kept coming, even as did the challenges.

Early the next morning, too impatient to wait until nine a.m. to make the necessary phone calls, I wondered if the Toronto neurosurgeon could refer me. I sent him an email at seven a.m. I deserved what I got for my impatience. His response came as a swift, decisive blow: *Have your family doctor make the referral and the phone call. Your search will never end, and you have to eventually draw a line in the sand and be prepared to stop there. I've seen these interminable searches ruin patients by overloading them with information and wasting time. I think it is time for me to respectfully step back, with best wishes for the happiest possible outcome for you.*

This email felt like a punch in the solar plexus, sucking the air out of me. Was I on an interminable search for the riskless surgery? Should I just give up and go with the local surgeon? I felt some anger and humiliation. I took a deep breath and recalled the qualities I had been given: determination, persistence. I recalled the story of blind Bartimaeus and the crowds telling him to desist, be quiet, and not cry out about what he needed. I decided I had not yet come to the line in the sand. I also realized I was profoundly grateful to this doctor. I could reply graciously, but this didn't mean I was giving up: *Thank you for your warning, your honesty, all your help, and your kind wishes. I see that difficult and delicate line between searching and accepting. I look for the grace and wisdom to accept what I need to.*

I then dutifully waited until nine a.m. and made three phone calls. I phoned Sunnybrook to inquire whether they would even consider me (they would; I just needed a referral), I called my own family doctor for a referral, and I asked the Hamilton doctor not to schedule me for surgery just yet.

As I was dialing the phone number for my family doctor, it occurred to me that I might have to make a case for why I wanted a referral to a Toronto

3. 2 Cor 12:9

specialist. Were there territory issues? I had no idea, but as the receptionist transferred me to my doctor, I hastily lined up my arguments, just in case I needed them. Indeed I did. She questioned me about every aspect. Who had given me this doctor's name? How did he *know* Dr. Bob had done a thousand of these surgeries? Persistence and determination were called for. But she supported me and promised to send the fax that day.

Later, when I found out that Sunnybrook Hospital had a worldwide reputation for this specific surgery, I was left with much to ponder. Did the medical people in Hamilton know of that resource just down the road? It was also sobering to realize that if I had been any less articulate, any less intelligent, with social or language challenges of any sort, there would have been no such referral. I had to fight for it, and I had the skills to do so. What happens to others with less assertiveness and less skill? I don't know what all the issues were. It was entirely within my rights, within the Canadian health system, to ask for a second referral. But it was not encouraged. I suppose that if everyone did so, the burden on our public health system would be overwhelming. Maybe in the whole scheme of medical challenges, a four-centimeter acoustic neuroma, a changed face, and loss of verbal capacity are just not a big deal. Whether it was Toronto or Hamilton, one hundred or one thousand times the surgeon had done this operation, my issue was small potatoes compared to others. But to me the potatoes looked pretty big. To my face, to my vocation, they did. Maybe I should just be glad to be alive, thankful to be in a country with sophisticated neurosurgery available. In many parts of the world, I would likely simply die, probably slowly. The Toronto neurosurgeon had described doing surgery in other parts of the world as "like with a knife and fork" compared to Toronto. I don't know how to respond to the questions that occasionally haunted me: Who do I think I am that I should fight for more? Why am I not content with what most people would simply accept? What makes me think I should have better? I am thankful to be alive. And given that the doctor of a thousand surgeries was only an hour away, I wanted to meet him.

Sunnybrook called back to set an initial appointment for a month away. I asked if there couldn't be something earlier. The administrator sounded surprised; this was already a quick appointment! She did offer something, though: would I like to be on a cancellation list?

That evening I emailed our two families and asked them to pray for a cancellation. My mother queried, "Who would cancel an appointment with a specialist?"

My son asked, "Do you pray about everything?"

The next day Dr. Bob's office called. There had been a cancellation, and my appointment was moved up ten days. That was my up for the day. My down was an email from my mother. She forwarded a newsletter from someone from my distant past. I knew she had continued to be in touch with him, but I was surprised to find "Cathy Stewart's brain tumor" broadcast in a letter he sent out to hundreds of people I didn't know. I reacted. I asked her not to use the language "brain tumor." Instead I called it "a tumor on the nerve that goes to the ear." The words "brain tumor" immediately make people think it must be impacting cognition, personality, and memory.

I was aware of what my reaction meant. I had indeed journeyed a distance. I was willing to be mistaken for a stroke patient. But loss of cognition? While I framed my objection to my mother in terms of how frightening the words "brain tumor" might be to other people, what was really at work was self-image. I did not want to be thought of as any less. I did not want to be held with the same fear or pity that I myself had attached to the words "brain tumor." I was not willing to embrace that humility. I was not willing to identify with those whose tumor *is* in another part of their brain, affecting personality and cognition. It crept too close to my core identity.

It also meant that everything about my journey so far, as significant as it had been, was nothing compared to the journey of those whose tumor does affect cognition. I was, again, humbled.

9

Biding Time

I read the Wendell Berry book you gave me. The most powerful story for me was the one about the old man who mends the fence and then isn't sure whether he'll be able to walk all the way home again. I really wanted that old man to make it home, and I felt that so strongly, and there wasn't anything at all I could do about it, except keep reading. And that's kind of what I've been feeling like for you . . . I have been treating you like Wendell Berry's old man, just wishing hard and waiting.[1]

WORDS SENT FROM A FRIEND, IN THE TIME OF WAITING

T HE NEXT FEW WEEKS turned out to be a lull in the action. I turned my attention to strengthening my body and mind and spirit for the great assault, though I had no idea when that would come.

I decided there was no reason I couldn't try running again. Surely the stronger and healthier my body, the better I would come through surgery. Ted and I ran together a few days, and then I ventured out by myself. I carried my cell phone with me in case something untoward might happen, but nothing did. I did not fall over or faint. The symptoms that had led me

---

1. This is a reference to the Wendell Berry story "The Boundary."

to diagnosis seemed to have almost completely faded. They had done their work.

In the lull, I even had time to write some poems. I wondered about the determination that had driven my ten-year-old self to that 1967 gold Participation badge, whether it was still there in me.

When I was ten

When I was ten
I ran a distance
under the eye of a stop clock.

I remember that 10-year-old's mind,
determined to cover the distance
in "gold standard" time.
I remember that school yard,
and the pumping of my
legs and arms.

Now the clock has moved
and so has the ground on which I tread.

At stake now is my inner fitness:
Have I grown a soul?
Have I exercised my spirit?
Can I wrestle with fear?
Can I hold my own
against a demon or two?

Oh ten-year-old's mind
Come strengthen me now.
Steel my muscles.
Pump my arms.

I need you now
childlike
fearless
confident
strong
to cover this terrain.

Through a circuitous connection, the name and phone number of a survivor of my same surgery landed in my lap. It was helpful to hear her story, mostly to learn how she coped. To read a list of possible physical side effects in a medical article is quite different from hearing a real person describe how she made her way.

Human beings, in general, seem to have an enormous ability to adjust. Others look on and say, "I don't know how you manage!" That is because we do not need to. It is not our life. When it is our own challenge, we often find resources we did not know we had, making choices we never thought we could. We really have little idea how we will cope with a circumstance until we are in it. There is another reason for humility! While it is true that crises reveal all the inadequacies we have been able to hide, they also draw out of us strength we did not know was there.

This is the story of the woman I only knew on the phone. The doctors tested her facial nerve immediately after the surgery before the swelling set in. Because the nerve was responsive at that point, they were hopeful that she would regain facial movement. But that hope was all she had to cling to for four long months. Once the swelling set in, her face was "like a marble statue" for four long months. Whenever she went out in public, people stared.

"How did you cope with that?" I asked.

"I just ignored them; I had enough to deal with, " she said. To me, that was a surprise and a comfort: it was possible to ignore the stares!

Then, slowly, movement came back to her face. Now that she was a few years post-surgery, no one except her doctor or physiotherapist would know for sure that she had a compromised facial nerve. She had 90 percent use of her facial nerve and could do all the normal movements: smile, frown, and grimace. One thing she could not do was blow up a balloon. As for the symmetry of her face, she now noticed that not too many people have very symmetrical faces anyway. They just think they do.

After the surgery she was off work for four months. When she did come back it was at half time. She struggled with fatigue. Her balance was quite compromised for a couple of weeks, and having a live-in partner had been essential just to be able to walk around. This was a story more sobering than the original prediction of "six weeks and then back to work" I had initially received.

I found this story profoundly hopeful. There had been four horrible months, but she had come through it well. It gave me an idea of what to brace for: I could handle four horrible months if there was hope on the other end. Ted heard it differently: four horrible months!

If I had not been the minister of a congregation, and if I had not grown up in the evangelical tradition where praying for everything was commonplace, I doubt I would have requested group prayers for myself. I can't say that I have any idea how intercessory prayer works. But here is what I do know: the prayer sessions with the elders of the congregation helped me. They gave me insight. They made me feel loved. They provided a structure for me to talk about my fears and needs, and also see how much there was to be thankful for. All that is surely good.

Some may ask: and if you didn't know about these people praying for you, would the prayers make a difference to anything? Part of me is indeed skeptical. On the other hand, it brings me great comfort to think of communities around the world (like Benedictine monasteries) who take on the work of praying for the whole world, some people by name, but countless others whose names they will never know, the recipients of the prayer never knowing they are being prayed for. I can't explain it. I don't think it is meant to be explained. I have a feeling that to ask how it works is asking the wrong question. All I know is: love is never wasted.

One Sunday worship I said something about "nothing is ever wasted" in my prayer. A woman buttonholed me afterwards: "How do you know that?" She had made an effort to reconcile with a family member and had been spurned. Was her effort wasted? I told her I couldn't believe it had been, but I could not tell her *how* I knew that. Years later, reading Cynthia Bourgeault, I was comforted to hear that I was not alone in this conviction:

> The great mystics have named this as the heart of the Mercy of God: the intuition that the entire rainbow of times and colors, of past and future, of individual paths through history, is all contained—flows out of and back into—that great white light of the simple loving presence of God. *Alpha* and *Omega*, beginning and end. And in that Mercy all our history—our possible pasts and possible futures, our lost loved ones and children never born—is contained and fulfilled in a wholeness of love from which nothing can ever possibly be lost.[2]

The prayer meeting required me to enumerate the gifts I was receiving. There was much to be thankful for—in the space of one week, I had received the referral for Dr. Bob, got an appointment and then a rescheduled one. I had found I could still run. I had found someone who had survived my surgery and was willing to talk with me about it.

2. Bourgeault, *Mystical Hope*, 64.

Sitting down at a prayer meeting to talk about my situation forces a kind of review. It focuses the mind and the memory. This in itself is a helpful kind of practice. It creates awe. I was awed that it was a conversation between two parishioners, recounted to me one evening, and then brought to mind because of a conversation with my physiotherapist, which led to a conversation with another physiotherapist, which led to the name of Dr. Bob in Toronto.

A prayer meeting also asks me to name my fears. Is there any point in this? Years later, in a book by Ina May Gaskin, midwife extraordinaire, I read that women in labor who can name, out loud, something they are worried about often see their labor progress.[3] There is something about opening our mouths and pushing some words out that does some good. It must be the mind-body connection and our need for human companionship. What a boomerang: we decide to be brave and speak, our vocal chords and mouth and tongue obey, the words are spoken and heard, and the impact comes back home to rest, in another part of our body. We are so much more than just a body.

So in a prayer meeting, I named my needs. I needed help for dealing with my fear of claustrophobia with only one working ear. I wanted the tumor to peel away. How was my family going to cope with all this? I still didn't know whether Dr. Bob in Toronto would take me! I was realizing it took skill to negotiate the health-care system.

Somewhere in the conversation, when I was talking about the woman who couldn't blow up a balloon or whistle, it struck me: what a grace that I play violin and not oboe or trombone. That's another thanksgiving—I am not an oboe player!

One elder commented on how well my path thus far fitted with the season of Lent, a kind of wandering in the desert. Indeed, my whole experience was taking on a strong liturgical pattern. My diagnosis had come just before the beginning of Lent. Serious wandering had begun on Ash Wednesday when I met the Toronto neurosurgeon for the first time, only to be deepened a week later when I met the radiologist. The wandering continued until Palm Sunday, when I turned my face toward Jerusalem (possible deathly things), so to speak. On Maundy Thursday the image of the boat/raft came to mind. Holy Saturday had brought waves of fear, appropriate for the day Jesus descended into hell. And by Easter Sunday I could talk about the raft that carried me through fear. Somewhere in this

3. Gaskin, *Guide to Childbirth*, 134–5.

season of Easter we began blessing the elders of the congregation, five at a time, so the church would not feel leaderless in my convalescence. They would all be blessed by the day of Pentecost, which, though I didn't know it yet, would turn out to be two days before my surgery.

Pentecost is the day when the church remembers how the Holy Spirit descended upon the quivering disciples, pushing them beyond fear into new boldness. Into what new boldness were we all being invited, I wondered? With what fears were we all being asked to wrestle? Maybe this was about more than the tumor in one woman's head.

I must have used the words "stroke of grace" in an email to my mother. I was referring to the appointment at Sunnybrook. She wanted to know what I meant. As I replied to her, the process of having to explain myself in writing opened up an intricate and mysterious connectedness in my journey thus far that I had not yet seen. What else could one call this but a web of grace, for where had it really started? Did it begin with a conversation between two parishioners about prostate cancer? Hinging on an insight about the role of postsurgical care-givers? How about the invitation to supper where we heard the story? Or was it the chipping day that led me back to my physiotherapist, who worked on my elbows but cared for so much more? Then there was a second physiotherapist, willing to talk with me. But the web would have been all for naught if I hadn't recognized the analogy between prostate and skull and taken hold of what was being offered. My spiritual director calls it a nudging of the Spirit.

Somewhere, somehow, I had heard grace described as a deep subterranean river that undergirds the universe. That seems to be the faith of the psalmist:

> There is a river whose streams make glad the city of God . . .
> God is in the midst of the city; it shall not be moved.[4]

Cynthia Bourgeault further develops the connection between grace, mercy, and river: if a river of grace runs through Creation, that very river is God. So that means the direction of the universe is toward mercy. But we can't necessarily see it. In trust, we open ourselves to its possibilities. We step into the river and let it carry us.[5] This sounds like Einstein's words: "I think the most important question facing humanity is, 'Is the universe a

4. Ps 46:4–5
5. Bourgeault, *Mystical Hope*, 29.

friendly place?'" He seems to trust that it is: "God does not play dice with the universe."

This is not to say that we always know what is good or that anything is purely good.

The Chinese folktale "The Lost Horse" warns of a flippant interpretation of what is good and what is bad.

> A man who lived on the northern frontier of China was skilled in interpreting events. One day for no reason, his horse ran away to the nomads across the border. Everyone tried to console him, but his father said, "What makes you so sure this isn't a blessing?" Some months later his horse returned, bringing a splendid nomad stallion. Everyone congratulated him, but his father said, "What makes you so sure this isn't a disaster?" Their household was richer by a fine horse, which the son loved to ride. One day he fell and broke his hip. Everyone tried to console him, but his father said, "What makes you so sure this isn't a blessing?"
>
> A year later the nomads came in force across the border, and every able-bodied man took his bow and went into battle. The Chinese frontiersmen lost nine of every ten men. Only because the son was lame did father and son survive to take care of each other. Truly, blessing turns to disaster, and disaster to blessing: the changes have no end, nor can the mystery be fathomed.[6]

What makes me think that this web of circumstances I was experiencing was one of grace? What makes me think I can call it good? I wonder if the quality we call grace has to do not so much with outcomes as with love. Each human action in this web surrounding me was one of care and love. No matter what would have been the outcome in terms of my surgery, it would still have been a web of love.

At the end of the week I met with an elder and friend in the church. He recalled the moment when he had heard what happens when the facial nerve doesn't work properly—drooling was the last straw for him. He could not contain his horror: "I know what I would choose!" I knew he meant radiation, though he didn't say it, and I replied, "That's what most people say." At that point he silently thought (but did not say), *And I bet she'll just end up choosing exactly what everyone else does not. That would be just like her. She'll not choose what everyone else thinks they would or she should. She'll go against.*

---

6. Roberts, *Chinese Fairy Tales*, 82.

As it turned out, he was right about what I would choose, and I was right about what he was thinking. So, upon hearing my discernment, he wasn't too surprised. He knew already. But he could also articulate exactly the contrast between radiation and surgery that I had seen: *radiation is all in your head, invisible, leaving you alone. Surgery is visible and tangible, something one can work with.* Yes! Yes! Yes! He saw! How amazing to hear other people voice in their own words, by their own insight, exactly what I felt. I was not alone!

It was a similar kind of strengthening experience to talk with another friend. She could see why I was choosing surgery. She could sense that God was present in it. But she had to hear my story in order to help her relax and trust in what was coming. Twice in her life she had been given uncanny experiences of unexpected gifts that came as if from the sky. She too had heard a voice speaking so clearly she just *knew*, and then was healed of something very specific. Her own experience affirmed that voices can speak what we need to hear. Again I felt the web: those holding me in prayer and love also needed to be held by me, so they could better hold me. The distinctions between sick and not-sick-right-now fall away. We are all in the same boat, really.

At the third prayer meeting, I was full of thanksgiving for the conversations that assured me I was not alone and for the teaching I had received at the Benedictine monastery from Sister Meg Funk, which seemed completely foreign to my upbringing. This Catholic spirituality (where did it come from?) coached us to move with the grace that is given. This was very helpful because it allowed me to go with my strengths and not have to take on the challenge I knew radiation would present to me. I could rest in "what you need has already been given."

There was one person in the congregation who queried: if the grace had already been given, then surely it was not true faith, because faith trusted in what *was not seen.* Hebrews 11:1 reads, "Now faith is the assurance of things hoped for, the conviction of things not seen." If I could see my way through the surgery with the gifts of personality I had since childhood, then how was this real faith? Didn't faith mean being absolutely naked? With nothing?

I had no counterargument for this. I simply had such a strong sense of having been given a gift. I went with that. There were enough unknowns! Was it this person's own fear of surgery that prompted the question? He likely had the same kind of upbringing I had: suspicious of a God who would just simply be *kind* and gracious.

I was concerned both for myself and for those around me. How would I make it through the dark valley that I now imagined as being at least three months of no facial expression and difficulty walking? Who would be able to walk with a weak Cathy? Would there be people able to accompany me through serious incapacity? How would Ted manage all this stress? I didn't know whether Dr. Bob would take me on. I thought of my parents, so far away.

I can't recall what these days were like. I sought solace in the woods most days, walking all the deer trails, crashing through the bush, in among the oaks and the pines. Ted, on a research sabbatical, tried to work on his writing. Peter still got to school each day, and meals appeared on the table.

The following week I met with Sister Mary. She asked me to describe the boat/raft. Until she asked me this question, it hadn't taken on any specific form. It was a metaphor that helpfully captured the difference between a decision and discernment, and the feeling of placing my weight into something I had come to trust. But it had no visual shape; all I knew was its capacity.

So I closed my eyes. The image that came to mind was a small circular boat, big enough to hold only me. There was no method to steer. I simply sat. But I was not alone. The gunwales of the boat were made of the overlapping arms of the people who had been walking most closely along with me on this journey. Their heads circled the rim of the boat. Keeping their heads and arms attached to each other was as far as this image could be called anatomically correct. The rest of their bodies were irrelevant because the skin of the boat was made of words: all the words that had been given to me. It was as if the words had been written on strips of canvas, and the strips of canvas formed the shell. This was the boat that carried me: words and loving people. I recognized the shape of the craft—it was a coracle.

IO

"TELL ME YOUR STORY"

When we are listened to, it creates us.

BRENDA UELAND, *STRENGTH TO YOUR SWORD ARM*[1]

A REGISTERED MASSAGE THERAPIST regularly interprets to me what she finds in my body. One day I said to her, rather out of the blue, "It feels like your fingers are dancing on my back." She responded, "Now the question is: is your back the floor or the dance partner?" I hoped my back was more than just the floor. At the end of the treatment, she said, "The texture of your muscles changed after you said that." In other words, that image of dancing, which sprung into my imagination, affected my muscles, making them more responsive, more pliable. She attributed it to the mind-body connection. There have been studies that show that when an image is flashed before a person's eyes, the cells in that person's body register a biochemical change. Our minds have power to change our cells. What we believe affects our health. Is it any surprise, then, the importance of a friendly surgeon?

---

1. Ueland, *Strength,* 205.

Dr. Bob was everything I could have hoped for. If forced to choose between bedside manner and surgical skill, most people would probably choose the surgical skill. But is it not possible to ask for both? A surgeon who can be both friendly and skillful is surely a better surgeon, if we put any weight at all in the mind-body connection. The way we typically prioritize technical skill over everything else reveals how little we know about the power of love. Any rapport or trust that can be built between the one lying on the table and the one doing the cutting will surely aid the healing process. Any ability on the part of the surgeon to allay fear, to answer questions, to help the patient feel seen and heard, to help her feel respected as a person, not just treated as another medical task, surely all that will increase the chances of a successful intervention and help the patient regain strength. To willingly place one's anesthetized body on an operating table is a huge act of trust. Dr. Bob knew how to invite and hold that trust.

Dr. Bob is an otolaryngologist, a specialization within the ear, nose, and throat field, dedicated to the study of the ear and related nerve structures. These specialists treat, among other things, facial nerve disorders and tumors that occur near the ear. Dr. Bob did only two kinds of surgery: acoustic neuroma and cochlear implants. He did one or two a week. He always worked with a general neurosurgeon, and they each had specific tasks, but he was the main doctor.

The examination at Sunnybrook was completely different from the initial examination with the neurosurgeon in Hamilton. The doctor in Hamilton had an examining room and then a "talking" room, which was like a corporate office, with a huge desk. The doctor sat behind the desk. At Sunnybrook, there was no corporate office; there was only the small room with an array of equipment to examine ears, noses, and throats. There were two chairs: one obviously for the patient, like a dentist's chair, and a stool for the doctor. I sat in the dentist's chair and waited.

In walked the lanky Dr. Bob. He sat down on the stool beside me and said, "Tell me your story." It took only four words to win my heart. I was a person with a story, not just another case of "glob of cells in head." He asked to hear the story.

He could hardly believe that with so few symptoms, I had received a CT scan. "You were very lucky," he said. Only about 5 percent of people with acoustic neuromas have no symptoms. I wondered what that meant—good strong nerves that could adjust? Could they now continue to adjust to this next disruption?

I told him I had already gone through a long process thinking about the options and had decided on the surgery. He supported that decision, saying that they are finding more malignancies fifteen years after radiation. In terms of the "do nothing" option, he was more and more discovering that many of these tumors were more unpredictable than originally thought. They used to just cut them all out as a matter of course. But now they did more watching and waiting, because they did not necessarily grow. Many grew to a certain size and then simply stopped. Why cut into someone's head if it was not necessary? Why radiate someone's head if it was not necessary? When they radiate and the tumor stops, is it because of the radiation or because it wasn't growing anyway? The research has not been done; no one knows.

Dr. Bob gave me some additional information about my tumor, gained through the second MRI with the dye. There was a cyst forming in the body of the tumor, which, being proteinous, attracts fluid. Even if the tumor did not grow itself, the cyst could, thus increasing the volume and the pressure on the cerebellum and brain stem. There was fluid collecting on one end of the tumor, also increasing its volume and impact. The tumor was starting to constrict the flow of spinal fluid in the fourth ventricle, which could lead to hydrocephalus. (A ventricle is a cavity, part of a system of canals that bathe the brain with a constantly renewed cerebrospinal fluid.) On the more hopeful side, the dye revealed that my tumor was not very vascular (not a lot of blood system in it) which often indicates that it is less sticky and thus easier to get out.

I asked about how he would gauge the risk to the facial nerve. I was surprised—his numbers were even harder to bear: 40 percent chance of damage to the facial nerve. I flipped the numbers to what really mattered: 60 percent chance of a normal face, as opposed to the previous 80 and 70 percent. It seemed that the more they knew about this tumor, the less chance I had to "save face." Dr. Bob did not minimize the risk: "We simply never know what we'll find when we enter the skull." When I asked about the possibility of a cochlear implant to regain hearing after surgery, he shook his head. I would no longer have the necessary bones in my ear. The loss of my hearing was the least of my worries, considering the other possible morbidities.

"You mean death?"

No, he didn't mean death. (I later learned what this medical term means: injury.)

He didn't seem to want to go into any more detail about other possible morbidities. I did not sense he was trying to scare me, nor protect himself in case of things going wrong. I sensed, rather, that it was a realistic assessment of the delicacy of what lay inside the skull and the human capacity to intervene. There were unknowns one simply could not predict. He did not, and could not, approach this surgery with any kind of bravado. It had to be done, and it could be done, but there was always risk. If technology had vastly improved our chances of getting in and out of the skull without too much damage, we were to count ourselves fortunate. There was a reason, after all, for the brain's multiple layers of protection: the bone of the skull, the tough fibrous dura mater, then two more delicate membranes called arachnoid and pia mater. The brain is a delicate thing. How fortunate we are simply to be able to do anything called good.

This stance, this attitude, I could only call humility: a sense of the enormity of the task, the delicacy of the body, and yet the call to act. It gave me a deep sense of comfort to be in the hands of one whom I could call humble. How fortunate and comforting that both my diagnosing doctor in Emergency and my treating surgeon could articulate so explicitly to me how their vocation called them to walk in humility.

We started talking dates. The administrator had previously told me that April and May were already fully booked, so I was hoping for June. That was no longer possible. They were now booking into the fall. My face must have revealed some disappointment, because she looked at me, paused a moment, and replied, "Well, hold on." She disappeared down the hall and came back a few minutes later. "Would you want May 29?"

"Yes," I said, without hesitation.

So it was decided: three weeks left of life as I knew it. She booked another set of appointments, to meet the neurosurgeon and do tests on my hearing and balance, and we were finished.

On the drive home from the appointment I continued to ruminate on the conversation with Dr. Bob. He had begun by saying I had three options: do nothing, surgery, or radiation. I had been so sure about the surgery over the radiation that I had only listened with detached interest to the new information about the "do nothing" option. Was he suggesting that I might actually do nothing and just watch it? Because it might not grow anymore? This would save my face and my ear! No one had actually suggested the possibility that we just watch to see if it grew. Queasiness in my stomach arose as the "do nothing" option started to eat away at me. Why go through the dramatics of surgery if he really didn't think it was necessary? I looked at my watch: it was four p.m. They had said I could call about anything. They were likely still there. I had a cell phone in my hand. Why not?

I pulled out Dr. Bob's office phone number and dialed, getting the office administrator's friendly voice. She started into a response, then stopped abruptly. "You know, Dr. Bob is standing right here. Would you like to talk to him?" He came on the line. We were already on teasing terms: "Is this you again?" He understood my question, and could answer clearly: he had outlined the "do nothing" option in order to be comprehensive. It was my body, after all. But he would not advise it. If I waited four or five years and it grew, it would be harder to get out. The larger the tumor, the more risks involved. Any procedure from here on would be "on the down side of hopeful." The waiting made sense with small tumors.

As I got off the phone, I felt an enormous satisfaction: I had paid attention to my body. It had been a perfectly legitimate question, and the answer helped me. Why spend a sleepless night wondering about it? This was another "You go, girl" action on my part: acting decisively, paying attention to the disconcertment growing in my stomach, and doing something about it. There was so much to learn about being a good patient. And how many neurosurgeons are just standing nearby and able to answer a phone call?

Somewhere on that stretch of highway between the hospital and our home in the forest, as he drove, Ted blurted out, "I feel as if I have a tumor in my head." His words hung in the air between us. I don't remember what I said in response. Probably nothing, but I received those words as a gesture of solidarity and compassion. He had been drawn into this suffering against his will, and while at first he had resisted it with all his might, maybe now he was surrendering to it, letting it find a place within him. He was not fighting it. He was on his own journey with fear, and occasionally I was given a glimpse of it.

That evening I wrote, *I like to put those two together: Sunnybrook and surgery. The one makes the other sound possibly pleasant, which it will not be, but maybe the "sunny brook" part will spill its grace upon the surgery part.*

As I lay in bed that night I recalled the number that seemed confirmed now: Dr. Bob had done a thousand acoustic neuroma surgeries. I calculated: "One thousand means that if he did even just one a week, that is close to fifty surgeries per year. It would take at least twenty years to do a thousand. I am in good hands."

I considered the next three weeks. Up until now, I had thought that even a June date was unlikely. Was it a good thing to get on with my life? Ted would have preferred that I hold off on the surgery until the fall and just enjoy the summer hanging onto all my presurgery luxuries. That was a designation for my present body that I had just that moment developed: luxury. Maybe I should hold on to what was good? But I'd prefer to recuperate in nice weather. It would be harder to recuperate in wintertime.

I thought some more about the morbidities. Was this Dr. Bob's way of reminding himself about the limits of his control and knowledge? Was it his way of wanting me to remain humble too? Not to put undue trust? Reminding me that he is *not* God?

I sent out the latest to my community, and they reflected back to me what they saw, which was a lot of good. I needed to hear that. I needed to hear that others too saw something good. I needed their assurances that all this good seemed to bode well. My sister-in-law reminded me of the story of Gideon. He was a hemmer and hawer, afraid to go ahead, needing every sign. Finally an angel messenger prods him to go: "You will rescue Israel from Midian with the strength now upholding you."[2] She saw what I couldn't always: I was being upheld.

Another message, from one of my Benedictine women, was more sobering.

About four days ago I had the most unusual dream. It was about a woman who was kind of forced to jump off a cliff. She bounced off the sides of the cliff a little and was injured, but then got up and limped off, injured but still walking. I realized the woman who jumped was you! Then, the same thing happened again, and the same woman (you) was forced to jump off the cliff again, and she jumped off courageously—kind of like a kid jumping off the high dive. Again, you were injured a little but got up and limped off.

This email made me weep, because the cliff part felt true, and I wondered what the limping meant. I didn't want to think about what that second jump was about. Maybe the first jump was about seeing what awaited me, or imagining it, and the second jump was about doing it nonetheless, even having seen. Now that I look back, I can identify more than a few second jumps. Life keeps presenting them, over and over again. When we stop jumping off cliffs, we die.

---

2. Stahl, *Beginning to Exile*, 158.

II

BUILDING A CORACLE

O Jesus
Be the canoe that holds me in the sea of life.
Be the steer that keeps me straight. Be the outrigger that supports me in times of
great temptation.
Let thy spirit be my sail that carries me through each day.
Keep my body strong,
so that I can paddle steadfastly on,
in the long voyage of life.

ANONYMOUS, "A NEW HEBRIDEAN PRAYER"

S AINT BRENDAN LIVED IN the sixth century on the west coast of Ireland.
Latin manuscripts dating back to 800 AD tell the tale of *Navigatio*
sancti Brendani abbatis (the voyage of Saint Brendan the Abbot).
Along with a gang of monks, he climbed into a boat covered with oiled
ox hides called a currach and, navigating only with rudder and sails, was
carried by the North Atlantic currents to discover a new land. The tale, told
from a medieval imagination, sounds fantastical. The chronology of adven-
tures is shaped around the church year: on Maundy Thursday they arrive at

the Isle of Sheep, on Easter they are at the Isle of Birds until Pentecost. But adventurers in the twentieth century have discovered that, far from being an imaginary spiritual tale, Brendan probably was one of the first sailors to have crossed the Atlantic. Currachs really work. Ox hides tanned in oak bark and permeated with raw sheep lanolin can resist saltwater, and a currach can travel from Ireland to Newfoundland by ocean current.[1]

The poet in my congregation discovered the story of Brendan and wrote a set of poems about the saint. To trust oneself to the currents, to the winds, and just see where they would take you: that is what the life of faith is like.

Our imaginations don't come up with things out of thin air. They need food, they need building blocks. When Sister Mary asked me to describe the boat image that had come to me, it was this story of Brendan, floating in my consciousness, that gave rise to the details of the boat.

Coracles are smaller and a slightly different shape than currachs. They can only hold one person, and they do not go out to sea. Their structure is made of woven branches covered with canvas or oiled animal skin and sealed with pitch. They once ferried people across the shallow rivers of Ireland and England, but now they are used to fish for salmon and sea trout. A paddle is used for propulsion and steering.

The image that came to me was some kind of hybrid between currach and coracle. Like a currach, I was going out to the open sea, at the mercy of strong winds and currents, but more like the coracle, there was only room for one person. I was going alone, and it didn't feel as if I had much of a paddle at all.

The more I let the image sit with me, the stronger it became. What if I made a small coracle using paper-mâché? I was imagining something the size of a twelve-inch basket used to hold bread. That wouldn't be too hard.

The fact that the coracle I had imagined was encircled by a group of people led me to think that maybe it would be good to gather this group together before my surgery. After letting the idea sit for a few days, I sent out an invitation to the people who had been particularly supportive to me on this journey. There was only one evening when the whole family could be together before my daughter left to go to Manitoba for her summer job. That evening was two weeks away and just a few days before the surgery. I only had a vague notion of what we might do—together make

1. Severin, *Brendan Voyage*.

the paper-mâché? I didn't know yet; it just seemed we needed to gather together in the flesh.

Upon receiving the invitation, a carpenter friend, who had already built a few boats in his life, went online and found out how to build a real coracle. He sent me the website that showed photos of people in England making them, and even riding in them. The idea of making something suddenly became a real possibility. We could do a scaled down version of a real one, but using the same techniques. It didn't look too hard.

The coracle image picked up momentum when my sister-in-law sent me what was singing in her head, which made me feel, again, not alone on this voyage:

> Somos el barco—Somos el mar
> Yo navego en ti—Tu navegas en mi.
> We are the boat—We are the sea
> I sail in you—You sail in me.
> The stream sings it to the river, the river sings it to the sea.
> The sea sings it to the boat that carries you and me.
> Now the boat we are sailing in was built by many hands,
> And the sea—so deep and wide—it touches ev'ry sand.
> Oh , the voyage has been long and hard, and yet we're sailing still
> With a song to help us pull together—if we only will.
> So with our hopes we raise the sails to face the winds once more,
> And with our hearts we chart the waters—never sailed before.[2]

The preparations of the actual thing began in earnest. An elliptical shape of twenty-four inches on the longer side was drawn on a piece of half-inch white board. Holes were drilled around the outer edge. Into these holes were inserted some green branches, standing straight up in the air. These were bent over and lashed together to form a webbed structure. Once the basket-shape was made and secured, the basket was detached from the board and covered with canvas. It was almost ready.

I phoned Dr. Bob's office to ask about banking blood. I was told it was not an issue: there is not much blood in this surgery. I couldn't imagine how there couldn't be much blood involved, but I didn't push any harder—how little I actually knew!

The complexities of other people's journeys kept intersecting with mine. The previous year, I had been invited to the hospital bedside of Jean, an elderly man from Africa. He had been in intensive care, hanging on

2. Wyatt, "Somos el Barco."

to life. He spoke a certain amount of English, but he was more at home in French. The social worker on the ward had seen the possibility: would he like a visit from a minister who could speak French? The welcome was enthusiastic. My French experience had not included the vocabulary of the communion liturgy, and I did not have the words to the Lord's Prayer *par coeur*. I hunted down a French translation of the Lord's Prayer and got the words of institution out of 1 Corinthians in my French Bible. With these, I went to visit him several times before he recovered enough to go home. I hadn't heard from him in some time, but when he heard about my medical situation, he wanted to meet with me.

I met with Jean in the hospital following one of his clinic appointments. He clearly had something very important to communicate. He had been praying for me daily, if not twice a day, and had received a response to his prayers: it is already assured that I would come through this *épreuve* (challenge or test) just fine. He didn't know the reason for the *épreuve*, but surely it was to make me even stronger, an even more brilliant light, to continue to serve God, to bring a message of hope and comfort to people. When I said that I would lose the hearing in my right ear, he came over, sat beside me, put his arm around me, and held up one hand to my ear, praying that the tumor would simply *dissoudre* (dissolve, like sugar in water) so I would not have to lose my hearing. Upon greeting me, he had kissed me three times. On parting, it was four, with the last one a long one against my cheek.

While I could not believe in the *dissoudre* part, and it actually came back to haunt me, I felt very much cared for. He was effusively thankful for my care for him and was glad to be able to return the love.

One whole day that week was spent in Toronto at the hospital doing the preadmission work. I first met with Dr. Bob. Maybe this was when we made the "initials on my right ear" pact. Next on the agenda was my first meeting with the neurosurgeon of the team. Removing an acoustic neuroma is an interdisciplinary surgery, with each doctor contributing in his or her area of expertise. Dr. Bob, as otolaryngologist specializing in things of the ear, would do the initial slow drilling into the skull. Once the area was opened up to the tumor and the nerve, the two of them would work together. Presurgery, the patient always meets with both doctors, and it can vary, hospital to hospital, as to who will be main doctor. This neurosurgeon did the same kinds of tests the other neurosurgeons had done, testing balance and facial movement. He was quite interested in my symptoms, asking more questions about my facial sensations and what had led me to the emergency room that day in February. At noon I went through the whole preadmission process, including an assessment by an anesthesiologist, who wanted to test the flexibility of my neck to assure that the breathing tube could go down my throat. I realized that I knew very little about the actual logistics of such a surgery: what would actually be done to my body?

By the time the day for the coracle gathering arrived, it had become clearer what we would do. I had read through all my email messages and cards, and, in true Lectio fashion, had chosen the ones that particularly jumped out at me. I printed them and cut them down to individual strips of paper. I added some selections from Scripture. These were the words that had been holding me. We would read them out loud and glue them onto the canvas. We would also glue, in a band around the gunnel, the names of people who had said they would pray for me or who had held me up.

As this day approached, I realized that such a ritual might be very important for my children. They had been pretty quiet during my decision-making process. They had done an admirable job of not inserting their fears into my process, but I am sure they had their own. I wondered if this event would be strengthening to them. Would all these beautiful words be helpful to them too? Would they feel included in the care? Would it help them to feel we were not alone in this? I hoped so.

The dining room table was the right size for all of us to gather round. The as-yet-unadorned coracle sat in the middle. We lit a Christ candle. John the poet retold the Brendan story. I told how the image of the coracle had come to me and how I visualized it. Then we proceeded to the reading of the words and gluing them on. I handed out the strips of paper to the people around the table, choosing who might most enjoy and be able to read each one. Who could read the Dutch *Van't concert des levens, krijgt niemand een program*? (For the concert of life, there is no program). And who was earthy enough to read this one from my friend Kae? *Cathy from Canada, one of my favorite people in the world. Holy shit. I will pray. I am glad you caught it early and the prognosis is hopeful, but I am scared. I will pray a whole lot.* Peigi couldn't stop crying enough to read her own beautiful words, so we passed them to someone else. Ted voiced what his theologian friend prayed for us: *The honesty to resist reaching for the security of the blackest possibility.*

All this reading took a good while, but the sum of all those words, all so unique, so imaginative, was like the patchwork effect of pebbles on the shore of Lake Superior, with their myriad colors, patterns, and shapes. By the time we had read all the words, we all felt very full, and there wasn't much energy left for the rest of the plan, but we continued. We sang the song Elaine had sent, "Somos el Barco," Ted read the prayer he had prepared, Carol offered a blessing and the sign of the cross. Then we had a party. It felt like a not-so-scared way to slip my vessel into what still felt like a very big ocean, as the Breton fisherman points out to God, "The sea is so wide, and my boat is so small."

When my Benedictine women heard about the service, they were enthralled, sending in their own words to be added to the service and the coracle. These words of John O'Donohue from the land of the coracle itself were amazingly apt:

> When the canvas frays
> in the curach of thought
> and a stain of ocean
> blackens beneath you,
> may there come across the waters
> a path of yellow moonlight
> to bring you safely home.
>
> May the nourishment of the earth be yours,
> may the clarity of light be yours,
> may the fluency of the ocean be yours,
> may the protection of the ancestors be yours.
>
> And so may a slow
> wind work these words
> of love around you,
> an invisible cloak
> to mind your life.[3]

It seems that the experience of journeying by water to an unknown place must be a kind of archetypal human image. I didn't really know it at the time when I took hold of the canoe/coracle metaphor. I had simply responded to what worked for me, but now I notice how many poems and songs express the same sense.

I had another form of encircling arms: the website TheStatus.com. This website was developed to help a patient's community stay informed without the family having to handle a lot of phone calls. I had never heard of such a thing and was, again, a little skeptical, but I was proved wrong again about the value of Internet technology. The Status became a lifeline to

3. O'Donohue, *Anam Cara*, v.

me while I was in the hospital. It kept people informed, but it also allowed friends and family to communicate with me and with one another.

The page on the site could be personalized. I entered the opening sentence from Annie Dillard, and also the French translation of Psalm 138:7, *Si je dois vivre au coeur de la détresse, tu me maintiendras en vie.* A literal English translation of the French would be, "If I must live in the heart of distress, you will hand-hold me in life." The French word "*maintenir*" is so much more vivid than the English "maintain" because it creates a picture of physical hands, holding.

Later I learned more about the original Hebrew word *chayyah,* which both French and English are translating. The verb *chayah* means "to live." In Hebrew, one can take the basic form of a verb and, by modifying its vowels and doubling its middle root letter, intensify it or show that the subject is responsible for the state of the person. So if *chayah* means "to live," *chayyeh* means "God is the one who gives life, holds in life, quickens, revives." This God does more than preserve and maintain; this Hebrew God is actively, personally making life.[4]

And then we came to the day of Pentecost, fifty days after Easter. The church remembers the story of how a little group of disciples, huddling together in a locked room in Jerusalem, overtaken with fear because their leader has been killed, is anointed by the Spirit. The story in Acts 2 has lots of interesting details (sound of wind, flames of fire), but most amazing, it seems to me, is how they are no longer afraid.

Earlier that week I had been rereading an email from another sister-in-law. She had been finding it hard to reply to my messages because they made her more aware of her own fearfulness. Her confession prompted me to wonder whether the life of faith is almost entirely about tending to our fears: seeing them, owning them, and submitting them to One who is more.

This conversation gave me the idea for how to take up the story of Pentecost with the children. I sketched out two pictures, labeled Before and After. The Before sketch showed a group of stick people huddling in a house. In the After sketch, the house had disappeared, and the stick people were no longer in a huddle, but all over the page, their arms open, their mouths open, smiling. The story went something like this.

"Before the day of Pentecost, all the disciples were afraid. They ran and hid when Jesus was put to death, and they stayed afraid. They hid behind

4. Dr. Gerald Janzen, e-mail message to author, May 19, 2007.

locked doors. After the day of Pentecost, they were not afraid. They left their hiding place and started speaking in a very brave way. They got into lots of trouble (put in prison), but good things happened too. How could that be? The Holy Spirit had something to do with that!"

"God does not want us to be afraid, and God gives us the Holy Spirit to move us from being afraid to being bold, so we can do difficult but good things. I imagine you have things that make you afraid. All of us have things that make us afraid. All of us in this room have hard but good things we have to do, and we need to be reminded of this story. I have always wondered how the disciples' fear was taken away. Where does fear go? Maybe it doesn't go away. Maybe it just gets pushed aside, or overshadowed, or shrunk down by something bigger and more true. Maybe God is simply bigger than anything we fear. Maybe we come to church to help us remember what is bigger and to choose what to look at: God or our fear?"

Showing them the coracle, I continued, "This is something I made that helps me keep looking at God and remembering God is with me."

I was almost at the surgery date, but the questions did not abate. Somewhere in here I found out that, whereas the Hamilton protocol was to do an MRI on the day of surgery itself, to get one final orientation to the tumor's position, the Sunnybrook people did not do this. I woke in the middle of the night fearing: What if the prayers of those wanting the tumor to *dissoudre* worked, and after drilling for two and a half hours, they found nothing? Could I ask for a CT scan? Could I plead for one? Worse: what if, upon finding nothing, they figured that they had gone into the wrong ear and went into the left one also? Making me completely deaf? The newspapers report such disaster stories. They are surely the medical exception, but when we are feeling vulnerable, these stories prey upon us.

I mentioned this to a friend. His suggestion: "Maybe your head is like a watermelon. Make a knuckle and tap the right side of your head. Now tap the left side of your head. Does it sound any different?"

"The right side sounds deeper."

"There you go! Trust in the path you are on, Cathy." I had heard such whispered wisdom at the back of my consciousness, but to hear it from someone else's mouth was a help. It sounded like the Ignatian wisdom, "Don't make a change of course in the midst of a desolation." But this also was the gift of the scientific mind, given when I needed it: in all likelihood the tumor would not simply *dissoudre*. In any case, I really didn't have much choice at this point. It was another juncture of choosing to trust.

What should I do on the last day of my life as I knew it? I went for a walk in my woods, visiting my favorite spots: the exposed escarpment rock, my flat rock, the row of four oaks, and the maple tree I could sit in. One black cherry tree splits into three equal branches, right at eye level, creating a kind of nest in the center into which I imagined a candle would fit perfectly. I called it my trinity tree. I passed by the trinity tree twice, stroking its bark, and picked up some garlic mustard along the way. I could have lain on my rock all afternoon.

> Hear my cry, O God;
> listen to my prayer.
> From the end of the earth I call to you,
> when my heart is faint.
> Lead me to the rock
> that is higher than I;
> for you are my refuge,
> a strong tower against the enemy.
> Let me abide in your tent forever,
> find refuge under the shelter of your wings.[5]

5. Ps 61:1–4

12

Surgery Day

Pity the surgeon who thinks he is only operating on your head . . . there will be thousands of heads, and hearts, that will lie with you on that operating bed on May 29. I wonder if he will notice?

My friend Peigi

I GOT UP AT four a.m. in order to take the required shower with antibiotic soap. The water I showered in came into our cistern from the roof, so it was full of all kinds of interesting biological matter. Did the water undo the effect of the soap? The more I hear stories about infections picked up in surgery, the more I realize this shower was probably not a good idea. Ted, Sarah, and I were at the hospital by six a.m.

In the pre-op room I was told to take off all my clothes. "Naked like the day you were born," called the nurse cheerily. As I waited for Ted and Sarah to be called back in, I did yoga stretching exercises. I figured anything to help my body relax should help. I was wheeled up to the floor of the operating rooms. That was as far as family could go. We said good-bye and I was pushed through the doors into a traffic jam of beds on wheels.

Outside Operating Room No. 8, the anesthesiologist and one of the nurses introduced themselves, and soon after, Dr. Bob appeared. Without prompting, he pulled a pen out of his chest pocket and put his initials on my right ear. I was pleased—he remembered our agreement. I asked (politely) about the role of the residents. His fair and diplomatic response: "It's a team, Cathy. No one is going to be practicing on your facial nerve." He knew what I was concerned about; again I felt heard. I was wheeled into the operating room, introduced to the people in the room, transferred from the cart onto the operating table. The last thing I remember was hearing the words, "Now we're going to give you something to help you relax." Later, I mused: so that's the euphemism for anesthetic.

I have no visual memory of the post-surgery recovery room. All I remember is Dr. Bob's familiar voice reaching through to me: "Give me a smile." What a cruel request. What is there to smile about, except, I suppose, that I hadn't succumbed to the most morbid of the possible morbidities. I was alive. I figured out the point of the request: to assess the state of the facial nerve. If I could pull up my lips into crescent formation, cranial nerve VII was working. I must have done so, because Dr. Bob seemed pleased. I heard him say, "Good!" and then I receded back into the fog.

Once into the neurosurgery ICU room, it was the words of Annie Dillard that first came to mind: "I am a frayed and nibbled survivor in a fallen world, and I am getting along." Some brown lines (the walls of the hospital room?) appeared, and it seemed to me they must be the ribs of the coracle, because they were moving slowly, gently undulating, which gave me the sensation of being rocked gently in water. I was in the coracle, its words surrounding me. Sarah and Peter came in and I tried to describe the moving walls to them. I said, "They're like Pillsbury Doughboys." I was aware of laughing and also, sensing Peter's discomfort, trying to let myself be lighthearted for his sake.

Thick bandages pushed down on my right eye, and the right side of my face felt numb. I kept asking, "Why is my face numb?" No one could answer. The nurse suggested it was because of the breathing tube. That made no sense at all. It wouldn't be until months later that I would get any kind of explanation.

When Sarah got home that night, she sent out an email on The Status. The surgeons were very pleased; they believed they got all of the tumor. She also reported that *My mom was still definitely under the effects of the morphine/anesthetic, and very talkative! She says morphine is fun.*

That was going to be the last of the fun for a while. The first night in ICU was the worst. I rang the bell because I felt like I had a full bladder: was my catheter not working? A disembodied voice grunted something through the intercom in my room that I could not understand. I said, "I need help with the catheter." No one came. I rang again. Again came a disembodied voice. I spoke more frantically: "I'm going to pee my bed." No one came. I saw a nurse in the hall outside my room and rang again. She came in.

CATHY: I rang twice.

NURSE: No, you didn't.

CATHY: Yes, I did.

NURSE: No, you didn't.

I realized, even in my morphine-drugged state, that this was a battle I was not going to win. I tried a different tactic.

CATHY: A voice replied by intercom, but no one came.

NURSE: Oh, that must have been another nurse.

CATHY: My bladder feels full; could you check that the catheter is working properly?

NURSE, *as she looked at the catheter*: There is nothing wrong with the catheter.

CATHY, *realizing this was another battle she could not win*: Well, all I know is my bladder feels full.

The nurse pushed on my bladder.

CATHY: Don't push!

She continued to check the catheter. I heard a gurgling sound.

NURSE: Oh. Maybe there was a kink in the line.

My bladder began to feel better, but I realized how utterly vulnerable I was, in a single room, with a closed door at night in a hospital. It was just me and this one nurse, her word against mine, her will against mine, her compassion against my need. I felt very alone and afraid, like a baby, absolutely helpless. If I could only make it until morning, when people I could trust would arrive. I started to pray. There was nothing else I could do. "How hard it is to heal within an institution"—that was my sobering realization. I didn't have just my own body to contend with, I had to figure out how to maneuver my way through the maze of relationships that are part of any human structure.

Nurse of Night One and I came to friendlier terms as the week went by. Because my room was right outside the nursing desk, more than once I overheard her talking on the phone with one of her children, trying to cajole him to do his homework, answering his questions. I guessed she was a single parent and her child was alone at home. I got a glimpse of what life must be like for her when she was on the night shift: she didn't stop being a mother, even with all these big grown babies needing her attention.

13

A Week of Whinging

Dear God, be good to me;
the sea is so wide,
and my boat is so small.

Breton fisherman's prayer

The next day, even in a morphine haze, I could absorb some of the information gleaned from the journey into my skull. The good news: except for the narrow spot in the inner ear where the tumor and facial nerve had to nestle up close to one another, they were not stuck to one another, which meant much less damage to the facial nerve than anticipated. The unanticipated: the tumor had been taking up more space than estimated because of the volume of fluid held in the arachnoid cyst on one end. The numbness of my face was because the trigeminal nerve had been affected. This was the first I had heard about thick cranial nerve V that ran along the other side of the tumor. The trigeminal controls all the sensation on the face: how the eye, skin, tongue, and teeth respond to heat and cold, pain, and pressure. No one seemed too worried about it; it would bounce back, they assured me.

Most painful was the neck and shoulder pain. I wondered what position my head had been in for those six hours. Then there was something dripping from my ear onto my neck: a cerebral spinal fluid leak. I don't know how a leak in the system would ordinarily show itself, but I had to ask, "Wouldn't my ear drum prevent liquid from coming down the canal?" This was the only time Dr. Bob showed a little irritation. He sighed and said, "We must have nicked it." They hoped the leak would seal on its own overnight, but if not, they would put in a spinal drain to relieve the pressure in the upper part of the system and allow it to heal. That would mean more time in ICU.

My next nurse was a garrulous Caribbean mama with two grown sons, both unmarried. She was my nurse for only two shifts, but it was enough to let myself sink into her care. She saw herself as my eating coach, but since she couldn't hang around to feed me, she commissioned my daughter Sarah to carry out the role. She obviously liked Sarah, but the next day, when Peter came, the true soft spot of her heart was revealed. Supper had arrived. My nurse-mama had ordered me the full regular meal, in the hopes that regular food would stimulate my unresponsive digestive system. I managed one bite of the tasty square of lasagna, then balked. "One bite is better than nothing," she cheered. Not wanting to see this good food go to waste, she eyed my visitors. In a leisurely manner, she approached my bedside, took up my fork, carved off one bite, turned, and in slow motion, offered it to Peter's mouth. We all watched, transfixed.

Peter opened his mouth and received. The fork moved back to the plate, pressed off another piece, and returned, for the second time, to the white boy's mouth. He opened and ate, accepting Chloe's overflowing mother-love. Two grown boys were not enough for her: she enfolded my boy in her affections too.

As Day Three in the hospital rolled around and the cranial fluid continued to run down my neck, my neurosurgeon came with his drain. After consenting to all the risks of having a needle inserted into my spine (small but awful risks), I curled up in fetal position and let him do it. The brain and spine are held in one closed system. The spot where the system had been broken (up near my ear) was the weak spot. By puncturing the system at a different spot, the pressure in my head would be decreased, making it easier for the hole to heal. If this didn't work, they would have to go back into my skull and try to repack the fat that was plugging the space where my ear bones had been. For four days I had to be mindful of a tube attached to my back and keep my body at no less than a forty-five degree angle, which was the most aggravating of all. It put all the weight of my upper body onto the base of my spine. It took weeks, home on my own $300 mattress, for my back to recover from lying eight days in a bed for which the hospital had spent tens of thousands of dollars.

Hospital drama (and insight into the health care system) for the day was provided by the neurosurgeon. With great pride, he explained how he was saving the hospital money with his simple tubing mechanism that cost ninety-nine cents as opposed to the $200 version that was the standard: "Just as good and no need for power. Someone in the health care system must have a family investment in that company."

A routine was established: my parents came in at nine and stayed until midafternoon, when family from Hamilton would come. My mother is the more verbal one. She had written to me continually through the previous months, and at the hospital she tried to keep a journal of things. My father hit it off with Dr. Bob, kibitzing about fishing in Northern Ontario and living in the Canadian prairies. Hearing the two chatter away felt like home to me. My dad could connect with anyone, it seemed to me. In relation to me and my head, though, much weightier emotional terrain, he was pushed into silence. He massaged my neck. It is not only by words that people are present. His physical presence was foundational. It always has been.

Ted came in and worried out loud about what would happen if this lumbar drain didn't work. My stomach responded to his worry with instant queasiness. For four days we would live with an unknown: would the drain work or not? We could live those four days either in hope or in worry—assuming the best or imagining the worst case. Which path I chose would make a difference in my quality of life for those four days, at the very least, and could well affect the outcome at the end as well. I was going to choose to live in hope.

A message sent from one of his colleagues came to mind: *What to pray for? Courage, the honesty to resist reaching for the security of the darkest possibility.* I now saw how the darkest possibility could be a form of security: it means you can't be disappointed. When you dwell in the darkest possibility, you can never be surprised by anything. You have braced yourself. You have made yourself less vulnerable.

Despite the addition of the drain to my body, Day Three was a better day. Dr. Bob admonished me with "No whinging," and teased, "At least I got a half-assed smile out of you." I even went for a short walk with support without massive dizziness.

The triumph for the day had to do with peeing. The nurses were anxious to stop the use of the catheter and get me to urinate normally. I had sat on the commode beside my bed several times, to no avail. I asked to have the commode wheeled into the washroom—maybe more privacy would help. As I sat there, on the commode, in the washroom, I decided: this is silly; why not sit on the toilet itself? My body responded to the familiarity of the toilet seat by relaxing and releasing, as it knew how. Clarissa the nurse was suitably celebratory.

I suspect this triumph also had something to do with the mind-body connection. There was obviously some connection between the emotional experience of familiarity and privacy, where interruption is unlikely or impossible, and my bladder muscle's ability to relax. This muscle could not relax at will nor respond well to commands. The body needed the mind to be at ease.

Every day, Ted or Sarah brought in the messages that had arrived on The Status and read them to me. In the hospital, my world had shrunk down to one bed, one room, one body. When the messages came in, my world expanded and I felt connected by bonds of love to something much bigger than myself. Those messages held my heart and made me laugh. My brother loved the story about the tubing: *A cheap stent is one thing, but if she starts asking for porridge and saving her juice boxes in a drawer to cash in once they let her out of ICU, we'll know for sure what's filling up that empty space in her head. "The latent Scot ganglion," I think it's called . . . rarely seen clearly on MRIs and X-rays but much speculated about in scientific and Gaelic circles.*

We have all heard the proverbial wisdom: laughter is the best medicine. This message from a friend in California I count as good as morphine: *I have this overwhelming urge to bring you a casserole or build a barn or harvest your soybeans or something (what can I say, I'm a Mennonite). Prayer and love will have to do across the miles.* There are so many ways to send love.

One of my ongoing projects, interrupted by surgery, was the war against garlic mustard. An invasive plant that had been introduced into North America from Europe, it is now threatening forests in Canada. It is prolific: one plant can produce as many as five hundred seeds, and the seeds last for up to five years in the soil. It monopolizes the forest floor through sheer volume, crowding out native plants and leaving poisonous enzymes in the soil that harm the trees. On walks with my neighbor Peigi, I had taught her how to identify it, and now she was the warrior in the woods. She entered into my experience through the metaphor of garlic mustard: *Now my thoughts turn to the holes in the ground left by the removed roots. With the invader gone, the soil has to readjust. The root systems have to realign so that the native plants and trilliums can regain their rightful places. Does the earth feel pain as it readjusts once the invader is removed? It has to fill the hole and settle once again in order for the forest floor to reassert its beauty. I look forward to the bounty of trilliums that will greet you next spring.* It was comforting to liken my brain to the quiet earth of the forest floor. That was a world I understood. Metaphors, I figure, are the fruit of love, the evidence of taking the time to imagine and enter into another person's world.

At the same time as I reveled in these messages coming in from all over the continent, I was aware of how cut off my daughter Miriam was from all this, on an island in Lake of the Woods, with one phone only accessible by party line, which didn't always work. There seemed to be no technology to bridge that gap: wilderness creates separation.

Day Four was marked by several short walks down the hall and some standing without assistance. My face was drooping, apparently, though I didn't look in a mirror: no time, no energy for questions of appearance.

Day Five I asked Andre the nurse if I could get a fresh pair of socks. "Yes," he said, then after a pause (in which he must have thought of how to ask the question so politely), "How would they be different from these ones?" I explained that my daughter had complained that my feet were beginning to smell. "Oh! Yes! I'll get you a new pair, but let's not throw these ones away. They're very expensive!"

I tried to retreat from my request. "How about we just rinse them out, then?"

"No, I'll just put the old ones in a drawer here, and you can take them home with you."

Thus I remain the proud owner of antithrombotic leggings, at a cost of what, I do not know. I was impressed by a nurse who cares about the costs within the medical system and took the time to have a conversation rather than simply deny (or meet) my request.

Each day I tried to take some steps. On Day Six, I wanted to try walking unassisted down the hall. I asked Peter to walk beside me but not to support me unless I needed it. He matched my pace. What was this like for a teenager, I wondered, to have the roles reversed, to help his mother walk again? He didn't speak much, but with each step it seemed his spirits rose: "You're going to get better, Mom! You're going to have a summer, Mom!" I sensed that it was all he could do to simply take in the experience.

Normally, the acoustic neuroma patients stay in the neurosurgery ICU for only one night. There are two private rooms, both positioned near the entrance to the ward, held for the post-acoustics who typically have sensitivities to both sound and light. My room was thus separate from the rest of the ward. But for one of my visitors to get ice or go to the wash-room, or for me to practice my walking, required venturing out among the other patients. That was a sobering experience. The other tenants on this ward were in drastically different condition than me. They appeared immobile, with pins or devices to stabilize their neck or spine or entire body. They were drugged, unconscious, or moaning. No one was anywhere near walking. They were recovering from surgery on a brain tumor, or from severe accidents that had damaged their spinal cords, or from diseases. I had never seen anything like it: tubing everywhere, the sounds of ventila-tors, but very few human sounds, very few human movements, very little human anything. Their lives, as their bodies, seemed simply suspended, waiting, waiting. There was only one patient's voice that pierced the ward: the plaintive wail of a grown man in barely discernible words, "I sound like a four-year-old boy."

It felt like an intrusion, but it also required some courage to walk by and witness those in such trauma. Sarah, by some kind of grace, seemed able to walk through the ward with serenity. She and some other family members had some conversations with a woman who sat by the bedside of her husband who moaned. As my world grew back again from its shrunken one-bed focus, I had to find a way to let those other people enter my expe-rience. I came to appreciate anew the depth of human suffering, the hard work it is to heal, how intricately fashioned the human body is, and how love heals. I prayed that love could embrace such suffering.

Night Six turned out to be my last night with the nurse of Night One. Ted had brought in the coracle and she eyed it with some interest: "It looks like a big hat!" This curiosity prompted a little more conversation. We were from Hamilton? She had visited Hamilton once, for a conference called Women Alive. Did I know of those conferences? Indeed I did—they were Christian events. Remembering my first night with this nurse, I smiled wryly.

On Day Seven the drain was clamped shut. We would wait to see if, with the increased pressure now on the system, the previous hole near my ear would hold or burst a leak again.

My parents flew back to Vancouver that day. With some time on my hands, I decided to try to contact the coordinator of spiritual care in the hospital. She was the daughter of my former colleague. My relationship with her father had completely broken, but it would be strange to be right under her nose for a week and not even say hi. She came by just when the nurse wanted to remove the staples from my head.

It is interesting how situations of vulnerability free us up. At that moment, the past dropped away; it was the present story that filled the room. I showed her the words of Annie Dillard that I had printed out and laminated. She was suitably impressed by their relevancy to spiritual care in the hospital: how great it would be to hang them in her office! Delighted that she was delighted, I gave her my copy. When the nurse came in to remove the stitches from my head, she held back my hair.

I was moved to the ENT ward, where I again was given a private room. The advantage of this room was a full private bathroom. The disadvantage: it was separated from the main hallway of the ward by a short corridor, with a door at each end. If by chance the buzzer did not work, it would be very hard to make oneself heard by a nurse.

At five p.m., with no sign of new dripping from my ear, the drain was removed from my lower spine.

Two hours later a monster bee was drilling into my tailbone. The pain was excruciating, and even though it was shift change for the nurses, I insisted we hail them down for some painkillers. I had one dose at seven p.m. and other at nine, as well as some Tylenol 3. The morphine seemed to be able to hold the pain off, but just barely. The nurse called the resident and reported back that he had no idea what might be causing this pain. I could no longer walk at all.

Ted stayed the night at the hospital with me, which turned out to be more of a grace than we could imagine. My buzzer was not working, and if I had been alone, with the doors shut, no one in the hallway would have heard me. Sometime in the night I felt I needed to go to the washroom. Ted had to half-lift, half-drag me. He was scared: was this a permanent setback? Would I never walk again? What was happening? I had no energy to be scared. I was just trying to deal with the pain. Nothing in this process seemed to stay the same for long, so I just had to make it through.

The next morning when the neurosurgeon came by, he shrugged his shoulders about my pain. I walked a bit, with the help of a walker, but was dragging my right foot. I could sense Ted's panic. "Can't you make it work properly?" he asked me. I felt as if I could, but it would require complete concentrated effort, energy I did not have. It was easier to drag it.

The next day was home day. Early morning, the neurology resident came by and suggested we go for a walk around the ward, thereby killing two birds with one stone: a chance to talk and also assess my walking. He matched my pace (slow), and I got the sense that he was in no hurry, which was a comfort. He offered the only explanation anyone had for this new twist: "There are a lot of nerve endings in the tailbone; it is possible they were affected by the removal of the drain." I could live with his "We don't know" because I felt heard and cared for. Sarah came and fetched me, and I went home.

14

NEUROTROPHY

Van't concert des levens, krijgt niemand een program.

DUTCH PROVERB[1]

We could not see without our tears.
They smooth their film across the eyes'
irregularities, a constant mending
of the tiny flaws that pit
the tough, transparent boundary
of cornea.

ALICE MAJOR, "EVE WATERS THE GARDEN"[2]

T he reprieve at home did not last long. The next morning my left eye went cross-eyed and Ted drove me back to Sunnybrook immediately. One look and the culprit was clear: the abducens nerve (cra-

---

1. Translation from Dutch: "For the concert of life, we are given no program."
2. Major, "Eve waters the garden," 67–68.

nial nerve VI), which controls the side-to-side movement of the eye, was acting up. It is a long thin nerve, which makes it particularly susceptible to pressure changes in the skull. Dr. Bob did find it odd that a nerve on the left side of my head was affected by the surgery on the right side, but . . . as he had said, piercing through the dura mater holds endless surprises! An MRI showed nothing abnormal, so it would likely adjust on its own. A hand-crafted patch was placed on my more vulnerable right eye so that I wouldn't be seeing cross-eyed, and I was referred to a neuro-ophthalmologist.

Since Dr. Bob didn't seem to be in any particular hurry to get any-where at that moment, I asked if I could tell him the first of three stories I had been saving up to tell him. Story One was "How I Got Diagnosed."

"Didn't you feel pressure?" he asked.

"Yeah, but there is more." I told him about the coincidence of the yoga class in the morning that had focused all my attention on the egg-shaped space inside my skull, and the sensation of flames in my head that had led me to Emergency a few hours later. Could there be some connection be-tween the mind's focus and the physiological symptoms that ensued? Might my body actually have been responding on a cellular level to the mind's intent gaze?

He laughed. "That's enough of your bullshit stories."

"But you've got to admit it's a good story, don't you?"

"Yeah, it's a good story." He never heard my other two. I was not sur-prised that someone so highly trained in a scientific manner would dis-count the more soft science of how mind and body interact. But since he had originally asked me about "my story," I figured I should expose him to more of its layers.

I suppose that "bullshit" is how many might regard this whole story. A voice that asks me questions? A voice that knows me? I was not surprised by his skepticism. I can remember the days when, even though I would have *said* I ascribed to a belief in the bodily resurrection of Jesus (quite a miracle in scientific terms!), I didn't even really believe in something more basic: any kind of mind-body connection. I didn't really understand how a full long intake of breath might be important to an ability to focus for prayer. I had no sense of how powerful the practice of mindfulness could be. I scoffed, naively, about the power of the imagination. Bodies were material, following the known laws of science. But now, when I read something like *The Canon: A Whirligig Tour of the Beautiful Basics of Science* by Natalie

Angier, I am taken aback at how unscientifically I approach the world. I can see how the scientific method and its need for verifiable proof would not appreciate the yoga story. On the other hand, scientists continue to work to prove the biochemical changes caused by emotions, and the history of cancer research[3] demonstrates (in my humble estimation) that scientific research is hardly objective. Much about our bodies remains mystery. How can we have faith in our current knowledge, knowing what we do about the history of science and how our knowledge keeps getting revised? I have encountered too many stories that point to unpredictable connections between body and mind, between material and the elusive immaterial spirit. Too many of our experiences have left Newtonian physics gasping. Why could it not be possible that focused attention to one's body could reveal something growing where it should not?

I suppose, though, the yoga story is just the tip of the bullshit iceberg. The other stories I would have told him attest to something bigger: a current of energy that weaves through the events of life, springing up, connecting, surprising, surging toward life and healing—all those pearls. There is nothing that can prove that. All we have are stories.

I couldn't venture with him the bigger story that continues to feed me. It was a day in January 2002. Our family was living in a rented house in southern France, on the outskirts of a village of five hundred, at the end of a dead-end road. The house faced north, toward the Luberon mountains, rolling mammary-soft hills covered with forest. I gazed out onto those mountains every day through the big window of the second floor of the house as I sat trying to write.

That morning I was trying to carry out my sporadic practice of meditating on Scripture. I was pondering "[God] sendeth the rain on the just and the unjust" (Matt 5:45, KJV). I don't recall that I was in a particularly prayerful mode, but I did launch a question to the deity so described: "Who are you, anyway?" I meant: What kind of being can have such equanimity to treat the just and the unjust alike? Who can love in that way? I shot the question over my right shoulder. I did not expect an answer. It felt more like a mutter to myself than a prayer.

The unimaginable happened, and I have no way to explain it. There was a response. Did it affect the airwaves? No. Would anyone else have been able to hear it? No. Since then, I have begun to trust that there is more than one way to hear and know.

3. Mukherjee, *Emperor of All Maladies.*

It was as if a deep rumbly laugh began to erupt from the Luberon
    mountains, from deep in the earth's core.
It began slowly, and grew.
It felt like it could go on forever.
It felt like it was the same laugh that had brought the whole world
    into being.
The best verb to try to describe the movement of the laugh is a
    French one: *jaillir.*
It seemed like the water Jesus describes to the woman at the well in
    John 4, "The water that I will give will become in them a spring
    of water gushing up to eternal life."
The laugh sprang forth, like an underground spring gurgles up
    from the earth,
from a source deep down in the depths of the earth.

This is the only way to describe what cannot be accounted for: something creative keeps *jaillir*-ing in the world, unpredictable, unexplainable,
uncontrollable, but persistent. It is the base of the iceberg, and I do not own
it. All I can do is give witness.[4]

A friend knew a local ophthalmologist who might see me while I
waited for the appointment with the neuro-ophthalmologist. I accepted
the offer because I had decided to simply accept any offers of assistance.
When he called late on Friday afternoon, his voice could not hide his lack of
enthusiasm: there was nothing he could do about a sixth nerve palsy. This
phone call fulfilled an obligation.

Having no idea of the medical value of such an appointment, I said,
"I don't know. They say that postoperative people have a hard time making
decisions, so I will let you decide." He hesitated and finally agreed: "OK, I
guess I can see you on Saturday afternoon since I am seeing some others
anyway." I did not know it, but another pearl was thus threaded onto the
collection around my neck.

The next day, looking at my wandering left eye, he reiterated, "Nothing I can do." Partly out of curiosity, and maybe to try to salvage the effort
and time invested in this appointment, I asked him to look at my right eye.
"Is there any way to tell if it is self-lubricating or not? How will I know

4. Only years later did I rediscover, with delight, Phyllis Trible's translation from
the Hebrew creation story of Genesis 2:6: "then a subterranean stream went up from the
earth / and watered the whole face of the earth." *God and the Rhetoric of Sexuality,* 75.
Years later I also saw, in reading Richard Rohr, how the question I posed is a quintessen-
tially dualistic one, that sees the world in either/or (just/unjust) categories. The answer I
got was beautifully unitive, sweeping away my categories of good/bad.

whether I need to continue to use the drops?" He looked at my right eye and immediately exclaimed, "You have an abrasion on your cornea!" As he wrote out a prescription for antibiotics, I ventured, "So, it's a good thing I did come in after all!" My bold words were met with silence. He did suggest a proper eye patch would be advisable.

Under normal circumstances, black eye patches are easily available at the drugstore. But a new *Pirates of the Caribbean* movie had just come out, and children and adults alike were snapping up the supply. Eventually I found one and went to church that Sunday sporting my black patch to match a size 4 black linen shift that I hadn't been able to fit into for years. I might as well take advantage of this hospital weight loss!

That weekend I took a long walk in the one-hundred acre woods, walking on my own two feet. How marvelous to be able to walk. I was surprised at the difference one eye makes. I had to slow down considerably, which was probably a good thing. I wandered, rested, and tried to relax my neck and shoulders, musing that here I was in my forest again, less than two weeks after surgery.

Early Monday morning, Ted was horrified by what he saw in my right eye and called the ophthalmologist's office. My four o'clock appointment shifted to one o'clock. Ted's horror was justified: the cornea was now ulcerated, but there was nothing else that could be done other than what I was already doing.

Surgery contains much more drama than the slow work of healing. Many nights I lay awake, pondering this slow journey. I was not experiencing what my careful research had led me to expect.

I Thought

I thought I would look like a stroke patient: eyes wide and staring. Instead I look like a war victim: eyes closed and patched.
I thought I would be dealing with face muscles that do not move: instead I'm dealing with face sensations that tell me nothing. It is a completely different challenge: I needed to protect my eye through a mental process (reminding myself to shield it) rather than responding to a sensory message.
I thought I would care how people react to my appearance. I don't seem to (too much else to think about).
I thought I would be dealing with loss of hearing: instead I'm dealing with much of my vision taken away.

I thought I would have to deal with dizziness and suture pain. I did not anticipate the more mundane challenges of sheer muscle pain, tailbone pain, and not being able to sleep. I guess this all goes to show that the body has a "mind of its own" and healing is one wild adventure. I am humbled, again, and trying to live within the demands of the body.

Thursday of that week Ted and I drove into Toronto to let the neuro-ophthalmologist look at my wandering eye. Little did we know how the threads of grace were holding me together.

East Toronto Hospital stands in contrast to all the other Toronto hospitals we had seen. In contrast to the luxury afforded to brain tumor patients at the Princess Margaret, people with eye issues sit on little chairs running down a long narrow hallway outside the doctor's office. The office itself felt more like an animal burrow, crowded with stacks of papers and files. One desk and one examining chair are squeezed in among the filing cabinets in the outer office. And the neuro-ophthalmologist was running late. When we were finally called in, this specialist took one look at my wandering left eye, but what he saw in my right eye (not even on the agenda) sprung him into a whirlwind.

In the following hour, we did not once hear, "You have a neurotrophic corneal ulcer." We only figured that out by going on the Internet once we got home. What we did gather, by piecing together our joint recollections of what he said, was that this was not an abrasion from some outside object or incident; it was a hole that had generated from within because of the damage to the trigeminal nerve which nourishes the cornea. The cornea is like a delicate flower. It not only needs constant watering from the outside to keep it alive, but also constant cell replenishment—corneal cells must be replaced faster than any other cells.

The neuro-ophthalmologist wanted to sew my eyelid completely shut in order to protect the cornea and give it some minimal chance to survive. He had never seen an ulcer like this heal. If it did heal, he would be sending future patients to me for hope. The trigeminal nerve is a thick, robust nerve, but that means that if it does fall, it falls hard. Had an ophthalmologist not checked me before leaving Sunnybrook? Had they not told me of this possible risk to the eye?

Maybe it was pure shock that did not allow me to absorb this new information. If I had understood and taken his words at face value, surely I would have let him stitch up my eye completely, as he wanted to. But his pessimistic prognosis struck me as hyperbole. I resisted it and took his second-best offer: a partial tarsorrhaphy. He put a stitch through my upper and lower eyelids about one-third of the way in from the corner and pulled. I could still see. And with that, off we went.

The experience of having my eyelid sewn up, even partially, even with my consent, gave me an eerie sense of connection when I later saw the movie *The Diving Bell and the Butterfly*. After a massive stroke, journalist Jean-Dominique Bauby is paralyzed. The blinking of his left eyelid becomes his only means of communication. The camera is able to create what it would have been like inside Bauby's body when a doctor sewed up his deteriorating right eye, narrowing his connection with the world to one eye. A dungeon door clangs shut, and he is trapped inside. We don't realize how attached we are to each of our senses until one is taken away.

This latest assessment came like a hit in the solar plexus. Even with the numbness on the right side of my face because of trigeminal damage, the doctors at Sunnybrook had been quite optimistic about the capacity of the nerve to recover. While they had told me to water my eye, they had not mentioned any possibility of an ulcer forming because of nerve damage. Nor did I remember anything about possible trigeminal nerve damage in all my medical research. The possibility of losing an eye . . . it was too much to bear.

We hit Toronto traffic at the beginning of rush hour. Not having the will to deal with two hours of bumper-to-bumper traffic all the way home, we exited off the expressway and went into High Park. I phoned home, trying not to cry, and told Sarah to hold supper for us. Then Ted and I walked, lay on the grass, ate ice cream, drove to the cheese store and splurged. We came home to Peter and Sarah waiting with a meal that had been delivered by some friends. I said grace, changing the words of Psalm 138 verse into the plural, "*Si nous devons vivre au coeur de la détresse . . .,*" at which point my voice broke, but I eventually continued, "*Tu nous maintiendras en vie.* It still holds."

That prayer felt like an act of stubbornness more than any kind of brave faith. I was simply not going to entertain the loss of my eye unless I had to. Or maybe I simply couldn't take on one more challenge at this point. Some forms of denial surely have their place.

We ate our supper in silence. Our plates emptied, Ted announced he was going to the computer to do research (on corneal ulcers?). Sarah sat beside me, moved closer, and took my hand. Where did she learn this ability to simply be present?

In the middle of the night I wondered: is the potential loss of sight in my eye that second jump from my friend's dream?

The next morning a friend drove me to my massage appointment. We pondered the contrast between Eastern and Western medicine. What would Eastern medicine have done with such a tumor? The West cuts and drills. Maybe there is a place for such intervention?

I left a phone message for the neurosurgeon. He called me back within five minutes. He disagreed with the neuro-ophthalmologist's assessment of the trigeminal's ability to recover, and thus with his prognosis about the cornea. "I've seen more trigeminal nerves," he said. Maybe this disagreement lightened my fear a little. The medical picture was not monolithic.

As it eventually turned out, my surgeon was right about the cornea, but the neuro-ophthalmologist was right about the trigeminal. Theoretically the two should be linked (health of cornea linked to health of trigeminal) but . . . as Dr. Bob said, nothing is predictable. Possibly there was some intrahospital or intradoctor jockeying going on. I will never know. I do know there has been no lineup of people at my door sent to see the miraculous healing of my cornea. I also know that such an ulcer is rare enough that a regular ophthalmologist did not recognize what it was. I conclude this was not the usual territory for post acoustic neuroma surgery, and I am grateful that my delicate cornea found a way to survive.

So maybe I take it back about healing not being so dramatic. At the very least, it is endlessly complex. That evening as I sat at the supper table, it felt as if my own private fireworks display was going on in my mouth. When I brushed my teeth, I thought I could, for the first time since surgery, feel where the brush was on the right side of my mouth. I called that high drama because it suggested that the lower of the three branches of the trigeminal nerve was reviving, which meant that the trunk of the nerve must also work. Looking back, I don't know what that was. Wishful thinking? The healing process is almost like a mystery novel, the way the pieces and clues emerge. The docs could place their bets on the future of my nerve: I could only wait and see.

That weekend I headed out into the woods by myself. I told Ted, "If I fall, I'll just get up again." I got distracted by all the garlic mustard, picked a bunch, carried out an armful, fetched the wheelbarrow, went in again and picked more. It was mighty fine therapy.

I decided to send a card to the nurses on the neurosurgery ICU ward at Sunnybrook. I suspect it was not the usual thank-you card. It showed a painting by Canadian artist Erica Grimm, a naked androgynous human form from the waist up, arching back, head up, arms pushing down and away, and the text underneath read, "To what do you turn when you find yourself stranded, standing on nothing."[5] Inside the card I thanked the nurses for their help and comfort and care. I hoped they would display the card in a prominent place so more people could see it. It expresses what I am sure many of the patients in that ICU ward feel, and those who sit at their side: stranded and standing on nothing.

On Sunday I received a painting done by a woman in the church. It showed a basket resting in some reeds at the edge of a river, and it was accompanied by this message: *Tonight I was doing a painting for you of the coracle being beached. As the spirit moved me along, I realized that you were perched in golden rushes. It came to me: Cathy in the bulrushes, your coracle being the vehicle of delivery.*

People who know their Bible can communicate in short-form with one another. The Bible is like a treasure chest. One simple reference, "in the bulrushes," conjures up the story of the birth of Moses. The Hebrew people were slaves in Egypt. All male Hebrew babies were supposed to be put to death instantly, but Moses' life was spared when his mother placed him in a basket of reeds that was discovered by the Pharaoh's daughter while she bathed in the river. She took pity on this baby and saved his life. He later went on to lead his people out of the land of Egypt, out of the bondage of slavery. This painting now hangs in my living room, reminding me every day of how my life was spared.

That week, at the last of my prayer meetings with the elders, I spoke of gratitude. I could sort of whistle! My medical experts disagreed! Whereas at first I found this perplexing, a clinical psychologist friend was delighted: "That's a good sign!" Disagreement meant there was hope.

---

5. The title of the painting is a line from a poem called "She Enters Into Holy Souls, And Makes Them God's Friends And Prophets" by Susan McCaslin, in her book *Locutions*.

How amazing that my left eye going astray brought attention to my right eye, which was much more in need of attention. Such are the meanderings of grace. Nothing is straightforward. Nothing can be finally evaluated.

Acupuncture worked! I had become pain- and drug-free!

The Status website had become not just a vehicle of communication but some kind of larger light. One of Ted's colleagues commented that "The love in those messages is palpable."

I nevertheless had some concerns. I wondered whether the congregation would be able to relate to a new and different Cathy: talk to me on my left side, approach me, touch me (touch seemed to have become more important given the loss of other senses), not be afraid to speak/ask. I only really discovered this need when I went to church the previous Sunday. The first person to approach and talk with me (always accompanied with some kind of physical touch) was the teenager in the congregation with Down syndrome. I realized, in that instant, not only my need, but also the irony of who can most freely give such a gift. In such a congregation, brimming with postgraduate degrees, we were always vulnerable to being led astray about our own importance. But if the only real criterion for discipleship is love, then graduate degrees don't help much. In fact, maybe it is exactly the "weakest," in worldly terms, who have the most to teach, and the most to give, as Paul points out to the squabbling Corinthians,[6] and as Jean Vanier so eloquently describes of L'Arche communities. That day, I needed to be assured that I was loved, and it was Kathryn's body, her face and her hands, that spoke.

Within just over a week from the original visit to the neuro-ophthalmologist in Toronto, the ulcer in my eye had almost completely healed. Celebrating four weeks post-surgery, I walked alone in the woods, departing from the well-trod paths to find my hidden rock where I could lie under the trees. I was surprised at how disoriented I became with only one eye. Maybe I could get accustomed to being one-eyed. Or maybe I would just get tired and exasperated. That day I felt the latter. The two-eyed reader likely does not appreciate this. Just try walking around with one eye.

In the message I sent out that day, I described myself: *three-cranial-nerve-challenged, sometimes one-eyed, sometimes cross-eyed, one-eared, sometimes wobbly*. Humbling.

A good imagination had not been on my list of what I anticipated I would need in my convalescence. But it should have been. A friend who

6. 1 Cor 1

worked with acquired brain injuries encouraged me to imagine the oh-so-fleeting sensations I occasionally had in my scalp as the healing of my trigeminal nerve: "Go ahead and imagine. It could well help." That advice, together with one dramatic story of healing through imagining that some-one recounted to me, prompted a new sense of my work: to visualize the revival of my nerve. I had an anatomical drawing of it to help me. This responsibility to participate in my own healing was a new idea to me.

At the end of June the right cornea had completely healed, with no scarring evident! This was great news, but my joy was muted by the warn-ing that another ulcer could spontaneously form at any time. When a week later there was no further evidence of anything going awry, the neuro-ophthalmologist concluded that there must be some nerve energy getting through. He conceded surprise. To be able to surprise him—now that was an accomplishment!

I mused about healing as receiving. When I had a neck-shoulder mas-sage the previous week, the therapist had coached me: "Try to re-create that sense of deep relaxation on your own at home." It was somewhat (but not completely) a decision, an intention. When I went to bed that night I turned my attention to my shoulders, realized they were completely tight, and turned to relaxing and releasing them. As soon as I did that, sensations began in my face, and I had neurological fireworks (gentle and not pain-ful) for about half an hour. As I lay there experiencing this, just letting it happen, receiving the healing that I assumed such sensation meant, I con-cluded that our bodies know what they need to heal and often can do what they need, if we just let them, if we just turn our minds toward letting them. So I tried it again the next day: I lay on the couch and intentionally relaxed. The sensations started up again, almost instantly. To me, this meant hope for the long-term health of my cornea.

I pondered: in one sense healing is work; in another, it's not at all about work but about just receiving, relaxing. What we don't know about our bodies. I wondered if alternative therapies are partly about letting our bodies find their own way of healing, by relaxing.

Hanging up the laundry one morning, it dawned on me: I must be one of the few people in the world who has an injured trigeminal nerve and who has the experience of feeling it revive. It is a very interesting experi-ence to feel waves of sensation across one's face, at sporadic times, every time somewhat different. I decided that though the numbness was irritat-ing and required constant vigilance, though it was somewhat embarrassing to have to be reminded of the food hanging off the right side of my mouth when I ate, though the absence of feeling evoked a sense of loss that could pull at me, I could nevertheless enjoy this unique experience. The sensations and jolts felt like a baby's kicks inside the womb: they were signs of the life within and its desire to stretch, make itself known. I would receive these sensations as the kicks of life growing within.

On a different note: one day I put the phone up to my right ear and concluded, "The phone line must be dead." Then I realized, no, and switched the phone to the other side of my head. That deadness has remained a grief I have learned to bear. I described myself as living in the midst of birth and death, as we all are, all the time, but often unaware.

During a church service in mid-July, my right eye started to blur and I couldn't tell the reason: was it junk in there? or another ulcer starting to form? Jim, an elder, came and sat by me after the service, asking how I was. I told him what was happening and that it worried me. He was quite emphatic: "Your body will heal." He continued, groping for an image: "Your body wants to heal . . . like . . . like a piece of music wants to get back to its home key."

He had just been at a weeklong chamber music workshop, playing Beethoven. A Beethoven quartet starts out in a home key, then modulates and wanders, and eventually returns home. The departure and the adventure of wandering are what create the tension and beauty of the music, just as the final return is immensely satisfying.

It was a moving and beautiful metaphor that the musical part of me could understand. He said it so emphatically that I decided simply to trust in his confidence. And, as it turned out, there was reason to trust: the eye did clear up with some drops and has remained good.

Jim's words have stayed with me. I pass them on to others. It doesn't mean that our body will end up healing, only that it wants to. That in itself is hopeful. When I told my mother the story, she said, "Thank God for that elder."

A few days later, at my regular ophthalmology appointment, for the first time since surgery, both eyes tested normal vision. The doctor didn't see any reason why we couldn't proceed with our summer holiday plan to drive out to Winnipeg and then fly to Yellowknife. The only medical intervention necessary during that time was to get some eyelashes removed—I couldn't feel them. A few days before we were to return, the entry point for the suture became infected. I treated it the way one would any other skin infection (warm salt water), and we finished out the trip as planned.

When we were back, mid-August, I requested that the neuro-ophthalmologist now remove the suture, as it was causing infection. I thought that would be the obvious thing to do. He surprised me. He was skeptical, still concerned the eye could dry out. But I stuck to my request. He removed it, and the eye has been fine ever since.

At the end of August, I summarized my medical situation for my community of cheerleaders around the world: *I continue to have lots of interesting but mostly transient sensations. They vary from tingling, to stiffness like a mask, to sharp cracks, to lines of moving waves. I think that permanent feeling is slowly creeping back into my face in a line heading toward my mouth (at the least that's the trajectory on the lower part of my face; not much change in the upper). When the day comes that I can feel the right half of my lips, then I'll know for sure there has been progress.*

My cornea seems to be holding its own. I put drops into my eye every two hours because I have no way to tell when or if my eye is drying out. Drops every two hours are a bother, but better than losing the eye! Nor can I tell whether the tear duct is working. I figure the only way to find out is to let myself cry, tears or not, whenever. Maybe one day I will feel the tears.

The eye and my face on the right side go red when I don't get enough rest, so I try to rest a few hours a day. I can see properly from it, and with the suture removed I can even bear to look at myself in the mirror. My left eye is back to normal; my balance is pretty good; I have begun to put on the weight I lost in the hospital; people tell me that my face looks back to normal. I am not back to running, but I can get exercise by lugging five-gallon jugs of water around our land in a wheelbarrow, uphill and down, to water the seventy-seven trees we had planted presurgery. They need watering because of drought conditions this summer. I plan to start back to work in September at a decreased level and ease myself in, as I am able.

15

Driven by the Left Brain

Prayer is a way of reminding ourselves to be who we are.
JEAN VANIER[1]

There is only one problem on which all my existence,
my peace, and my happiness depend:
to discover myself in discovering God.
If I find Him I will find myself
and if I find my true self I will find Him.
THOMAS MERTON[2]

This chapter is about me trying to understand, in some theological way, which is maybe a left-brain way, how a voice saying a few words ("What would you need?") could have such power to take away fear. Not everyone has this question. Maybe it is mostly mine and

1. Vanier, as quoted in Brown, "Doing the Work of the Heart," para. 27.
2. Merton, as quoted in Benner, *Gift of Being Yourself*, 3.

those who have grown up with the sin anthropology: "We are so sinful, what could trusting yourself have to do with God?" Hopefully, though, it also explores and illuminates something about the heart of the Christian gospel: God delights in human beings, and Jesus is a compelling expression of that delight.

Jill Bolte Taylor, brain scientist, describes how she discovered the right half of the brain. It wasn't in a lab, dissecting tissue. It wasn't through a microscope. She discovered it when she lost her left brain to a stroke.[3] With her left brain incapacitated, she entered a world she didn't ever want to leave. People came into her hospital room; she had no idea who they were or what their role. Words, titles, letters after their names meant nothing. She could only evaluate people by the energy they exuded, by their love and attention. She knew she liked the friendly one who came into her hospital room and snuggled into her bed beside her, but she couldn't have told you why, nor did she care to try. She simply enjoyed and trusted in the experience of being held and loved.

The powers of her analytical, logical left brain, the foundation of her career up until that point, lost their appeal. And yet, she was drawn back into its world. She learned how to read again; she learned the word to attach to that warm being who had climbed into bed with her: "mother." And eventually, she regained enough of her left brain to be able to tell us about her right.

The brain is still a vast mystery. As more research is done, a simple left-right brain distinction is too crude; the two parts of the brain are intimately connected and dependent on one another. Nevertheless, as Jill Bolte Taylor's experiences show, the lobes are distinct, and maybe this distinction suggests at least partially a way to understand Lectio Divina. I am going to use the left-right distinction as a kind of metaphor for the variety of ways a human being can know and perceive. Lectio Divina leads us into other parts of ourselves we didn't even know we had, so overshadowed have they become by our analytical mode. We have experiences that cannot be analyzed or understood in linear fashion, experiences that the left brain cannot explain. And yet it wants to; it is not easily silenced. So a wild conversation arises between different parts of ourselves, parts that really don't know one another much at all. It is as if they are almost strangers, introduced at a dinner party: "You're Cathy? I thought I was Cathy." Perhaps in that

---

3. Taylor, *My Stroke of Insight.*

conversation, we become more whole; we become knit together, because these brains are both part of who we are.

Though I believe my experience at the opera was more than simply a right brain experience, it certainly drew on all that the right brain had to offer. I discovered something very deep, very true, which contained huge affective power. But my left brain was troubled. My left brain could not explain what had happened and was thus vulnerable to all the other left brains in the world that wanted some explanation. Just as Dr. Jill slowly regained her left-brain capacity and was thus able to explain in left-brain kinds of ways what she had discovered, telling a story to amaze us, so too my left brain needed to catch up with what my right brain knew. Without my left brain on board in some way, the right-brain knowledge could be undermined by the tremendously powerful left, my own and others.'

Maybe it was my left brain's need to understand, its need to name what had happened, that drove me back to the Benedictine monastery in Indiana five months after the surgery. Sister Meg Funk was leading a retreat on Lectio Divina. Though I had been practicing Lectio for a number of years and had learned to do it in a number of ways, I had the sense that there was more to it. Indeed there was.

Lectio is about listening to a text. The text can be a written word, like Scripture, but it can also be something in nature or in our life experience. Lectio can be practiced as an exercise for ten or twenty minutes a day with a selection of Scripture, but in the deepest sense, it is a way of life. You choose a text or, more likely, it chooses you: "You will know what text," Sister Meg says. "You listen to that text until it is finished. You will know when it is finished. And then you move on to the next one."

In other words, you might have an experience, or a question, upon which you do Lectio for years. You explore it in every way possible, from every possible angle, with every possible sense, until it yields its gifts. Sister Meg alluded to her own experience of nearly drowning. She did Lectio on that text for years. Since then she has published the story of that experience, twenty-five years after the event.[4] Her description is not simply about the event, but it holds the fruit of all the reflection on that experience: what was the meaning of it? There are many life experiences, or themes, or questions, that are worthy of years of listening.

My left brain was floored by Sister Meg. How can you just know what text? And how can you know when it is finished? But when I looked at my

4. Funk, *Into the Depths*.

own story, I saw what she meant. The journey to that decisive moment at the opera, when the voice asked, "What would you need?," had been a Lectio journey, done entirely intuitively. I had no idea that I was doing Lectio. I had no name for the shape of it. I didn't even know you *could* do Lectio on a medical decision. So my process was completely unwitting, but also completely led—not only by my right brain, but also by a sense even deeper than that, which I neither understood nor controlled. During that season of Lent, when I had felt simply lost, wandering aimlessly, as if in a desert, going around in circles with no signposts, I was actually moving intuitively through four different kinds of knowing, getting closer and closer to that still center point of knowing through my mystical sense.

The realization that I had done Lectio intuitively suggests that it is a deeply human process, maybe embedded in the cells of our bodies. I was simply doing what a human being needs to do. It is not some artificial construction, some good idea. It arises out of who we are, at our most profound level. I find that both amazing and comforting.

For this retreat at the monastery, we were to choose a text and listen to it for the duration of the time. We would study it with our logical sense. Each morning we had an hour in the art room. This was to give us time to explore our text with our aesthetic sense. We would pray with it (this was the ascetic sense). And we would do nothing (spiritual sense).

I knew my text. It was the experience at the opera. It had been decisive for me being able to move forward without fear. And I now also knew that it was an experience that had come through my mystical sense. But I was still troubled by the question one parishioner had asked me: if the voice simply pointed me to what I knew about myself, then I wasn't really trusting in God. Rather, I was simply trusting in myself and my own capacities. That, he figured, was not necessarily faith, because faith had to do with trusting in God. His objection was really: "It's all about you."

Was it? Was it all about just trusting in myself? Some form of self-confidence? Some form of self-help in religious garb? Can there be a difference between trusting in oneself in a humanistic sense and trusting in oneself because of a conversation with Christ?

His objection (I realize now) was rooted in a belief about the transcendent nature of God. God is totally other. Human beings are fallible and limited. God and humanity don't mix, like oil and water (except in Jesus? But he's one of a kind, we are told!). He was essentially questioning whether *the voice* could have been "of God," because God would not invite me to trust in myself. Therefore this experience could not be anything sacred or holy or blessed or special or trustworthy or amazing if it was just about knowing myself. It was a theological question about the nature of God, and I had no answer for him.

Further, even if the voice was pointing me to myself, how did knowing myself take away the fear? Nothing, after all, had changed in the outer, verifiable circumstances. There was still a tumor in my head, pressing on my brain stem. It was big. Maybe it was even getting bigger. The surgery was still dangerous. The team doing the surgery was made up of fallible human beings. The whole endeavor still held morbidities unknown. Dr. Bob in no way minimized the risks; in fact, he put them even higher. So on that level, I should still have been afraid. Knowing that I had certain personality characteristics that would help me to cope with the aftermath, how should that take away the fear? It didn't make sense. And I wanted to make sense of it. The question nagged, and I had to pay attention to this nagging.

In her little book *Mystical Hope*, Cynthia Bourgeault describes the fullness of God in which we are all held as "mercy." Drawing on her reading of Helen Luke, she says, "The Mercy is first and foremost the great weaver, collecting and binding the scattered and broken parts of our lives in a tapestry of divine love."[5] Maybe this is what my left brain nagged for: to be woven together with the rest of me. It didn't want to be left out; it wanted to have a place in the fabric. If what I knew at the opera was held somewhere deep down in my body, that deep knowledge wanted to work its way up again, up to my cerebral cortex, so I could have ideas to account for what I had come to know.

Lectio Divina allows for this constant movement of connecting the different parts of ourselves. Maybe it is the ongoing act of knitting us together, a knitting that began at our conception ("You knit me together in my mother's womb" of Psalm 139) and continues our whole life long. Maybe the One who looked at the new creation, a human being with both right- and left-brain halves, and said, "Oh, this is very good!" wants the knitting to keep going. Maybe Lectio Divina is a way of continuing the work of creation.[6]

---

5. Bourgeault, *Mystical Hope*, 24.

6. James Alison, Catholic theologian, explores this idea of the continuation of creation in a number of places. He interprets Jesus' healing of the blind man in John 9 in this way in his essay "the man blind from birth and the Creator's subversion of sin" in *Faith Beyond Resentment*.

Driven by the nagging, I set about my work. It was much easier to do the logical part, to analyze and categorize: I made a chronological list of all the pearls I had received leading up to the giant pearl at the opera. In art time I drew strings of pearls and repeated body shapes with pearls around them. In prayer, I held each pearl and gave thanks for it. I brought the whole experience of those months back to mind.

I saw the graciousness of the question at the opera: it had turned me toward what I knew. Without the voice, I would have known what I feared: I feared the radiation. But that knowledge didn't allow me to move toward the surgery. It was only the voice that allowed me to move toward the surgery. The fear question would have moved me from a greater fear to a lesser fear, but my action would still have revolved around fear. The voice's question allowed me to move toward gift. It was what I *did* know that carried me into the unknown, allowing me to push off from the shore and enter the rough water. I learned later that looking at what we have, rather than what we don't, is the key to community building.[7] Maybe it's the key to just about anything creative.

> I know that in life or death
> I am held.
> As a river is held
> by the granite rock on either side
> so I am held.
> As I was held as a child
> in a granite palm
> so I am held.
> As a currach of ash and leather
> can travel across the ocean
> against the nay-saying
> of many an expert
> so I can be carried.

This retreat process was giving me good insight, but it still didn't feel as if my question—"Was this experience about faith in God or faith in myself?"—had been answered. By about the fourth day, my anxiety was rising. The intensity of my "being troubled" was increasing rather than decreasing. What if there was no answer? What if the experience at the opera, of being met, and knowing something, was simply a once-in-a-lifetime thing, and

---

7. Block, *Community*.

there would never be any such knowing ever again? What if I would have to live with this nagging, unsettling question forever?

I asked for an appointment with Sister Meg to talk about this. She couldn't free up a time to see me for a few days, which maybe was a good thing. Could she have answered this question for me? In the middle of that night, I woke and prayed yet again. I felt like I was shaking and maybe even kicking at a stubborn bubble gum machine; I had deposited my coin but it would not yield its treasure. Then four words came to me: "The voice knew you."

I instantly knew that a life-long prayer had been answered, though I didn't know it had been a prayer until that moment. I would have called it a longing. Somewhere in my childhood, when I was old enough to realize there were things about myself I had to hide, things I wanted no one to know, I realized that the most precious thing to me in all the world would be to be both known and loved, at the same time. To be known but not loved: what good is that? Or the reverse: to be loved for what I am not would be a sham. In that moment of insight I was given what I am tempted to call a taste of heaven, for surely this kind of knowing and loving is fully experienced only in relationship with God. Our human capacity for partial knowledge and stumbling love is good, but a desire had been planted in me for something more.

My spiritual director has observed that "being known" is key for me. I remember when a male elder in the church, who seemed to function as a body guard for my colleague, came and verbally pummeled me. I was responsible for the church's troubles, according to him. For weeks I suffocated under his words. I couldn't find a way out from under them. Someone suggested I imagine placing him in a bottle and putting him on a shelf. It didn't work. He punched his way through the glass. Then, finally, somehow it dawned on me: "He doesn't know me as God knows me. He doesn't love me as God loves me." So I started a mantra: "He doesn't know me; he doesn't love me; he is not God. He doesn't know me; he doesn't love me. He is not God." I had unwittingly stumbled into both the heart of human temptation (to make a human being into a god) and the only protection against it: to trust that a loving God knows me.

Now here I was trying to understand why this voice had such power. How had the voice at the opera given such peace? How had it been able to cut through the impossible quandary I had been in? What had the voice known about me? My four qualities that would somehow suit me for surgery? Or a deeper truth: I needed to hear the voice. I needed to be spoken to. I needed to feel known. I needed to be met. The answer was written on the top of the handout Sister Meg gave us on the first day of the retreat: "Lectio is about encounter: an encounter with God that changes us irrevocably." I had been encountered by One who knew me intimately, and that One had loved and blessed me. I had been changed.

If the deepest truth about us as human beings is that we are made for communion,[8] then at the deepest level, what we need most in our lives is some kind of experience of communion. And that is what the fourth level of Lectio is about: communion. It is about knowing and being known. It is about being spoken to in exquisitely intimate ways. It was as if the Gentle Physician, the one who broods over our conception and carries us from the womb, spoke to me, and I heard. Being spoken to transforms us, just the way Mary Magdalene was transformed when the one she thought was the gardener outside the tomb spoke her name, "Mary!"

There are two aspects to this experience: the voice that addresses, and the content. Even though the *content* of the conversation at the opera was apparently about me, the *tenor* of the content (the voice that carried it) was *other*. And the *other* reached through to Cathy and spoke. My detractor was paying attention only to the content. That is understandable: he was not the one being addressed. All he had was the content.

But the content is crucial. A voice only interested in transcendent power might have said, "Trust me! I can do all things!" But that would not have necessarily helped me at that point, and that is not what the voice said. I understood the voice as pointing me to what I knew about myself: "It's OK to trust in who you are. Who you are is what you have been given. And I made you that way and pronounced it good!" There was nothing moral at stake between the choices of surgery and radiation and what personal characteristics would be necessary to get through them. There was nothing particularly earth-shattering about the question "What would you need?" So really, the content of the message was not all that significant. But

---

8. Jones, *Embodying Forgiveness*, 114. Jones is not saying anything new; he is drawing on the early church fathers. But it was his articulation, in the context of discussing forgiveness, that helped me understand the meaning of that old theology.

it was nevertheless a profound and very down-to-earth affirmation. I call this *other* the living Christ, graciously accommodating my capacity at that point. The voice met me at a place where I could hear, thus leading me to trust in what I knew about myself and at the same time to trust the voice. It was a huge message of grace, healing a long history of subtle messages that said, "Do not trust in yourself, because the deepest truth about yourself is your sin."

Since this epiphany, I have stumbled upon a few acceptably left-brain accounts to my quandary (how could God tell me to trust in myself?). At this point of writing, I feel almost foolish to admit that this has been such a quandary for me; it seems that there must be lots of people who would immediately have understood the voice's affirmation of my being. But I had not met those people. And maybe until I had the experience, I would not have known what to ask of them or what they had to teach me.[9] It seems that this question of "God in us?" has only recently pressed upon us with renewed vigor in North America, thanks to a revived interest in contemplative prayer.[10] I turn to Evelyn Underhill speaking from the philosophical perspective, David Benner from a psychological perspective, and Lytta Basset from a biblical and theological perspective.

Evelyn Underhill helped with the theological question about the nature of God: could God have been the source of the words at the opera? Historically there have been two theories by which God has been conceived and presented: the theory of immanence and the theory of emanations.[11] Both are present and necessary throughout Christian thought. The theory of emanations postulates "the complete separation of the human and the divine; the temporal and the eternal worlds."[12] God is inaccessible.

In tension with this is the theory of immanence:

> The quest of the Absolute is . . . a realization of something which is implicit in the self and in the universe: an opening of the eyes of

---

9. This seems to be how we learn. We can encounter an idea and understand it with our left brain, but we may not know the truth of it until we experience it in some visceral or relational way. The idea looks quite different, even unrecognizable, from that new angle. For instance, I had read (many times!) the words in John's gospel about God dwelling in us, but I couldn't know the truth of it, or the implications of it, without an experience of that indwelling.

10. Bourgeault addresses this phenomenon in *Mystical Hope*, Chapter 2, particularly pages 35 and 50.

11. Underhill, *Mysticism*, Chapter V Part I.

12. Ibid., 98.

the soul upon the Reality in which it is bathed. For them earth is literally 'crammed with heaven.' . . . The Absolute Whom all seek does not hold Himself aloof from an imperfect material universe, but dwells within the flux of things: stands as it were at the very threshold of consciousness and knocks, awaiting the self's slow discovery of her treasures.[13]

This immanence is exquisitely expressed in the New Testament by Paul's speech at the Areopagus, "He is not far from each one of us. For 'In Him we live and move and have our being,'"[14] and in the gospel of John, "This is the Spirit of truth. . . . You know him, because he abides with you, and he will be in you. . . . On that day you will know that I am in my Father, and you in me, and I in you."[15]

This experience of God as immanent is evident in the life of Teresa of Avila, from the sixteenth century, who says, "You find God in yourself and yourself in God." Or Meister Eckhart: "We are all meant to be mothers of God. What good is it to me if this eternal birth of the divine Son takes place unceasingly, but does not take place within myself? And, what good is it to me if Mary is full of grace if I am not also full of grace? What good is it to me for the Creator to give birth to his Son if I do not also give birth to him in my time and my culture? Then, then is the fullness of time: When the Son of Man is begotten in us."

Cynthia Bourgeault, a more modern mystic, describes a basis for hope that goes much deeper than circumstance: "You wake up inside a warm-hearted and purposive intelligence, a coherence of which *you yourself are part of the expression*" (italics mine).[16] The trio of Matthew Linn, Dennis Linn, and Sheila Fabricant Linn state explicitly what I never heard as a child: "Jesus encouraged people to trust their own experience."[17]

Evelyn Underhill says that the theory of immanence has been dominant in modern theology. Perhaps that is so. Perhaps the evangelical culture in which I grew up was a kind of microculture reacting to this suspiciously humanistic-sounding idea. Richard Rohr, however, believes that this whole stream of mysticism has been quite squelched in Western Christian tradition. Given what he sees as a most unfortunate paucity of teaching in

13. Ibid., 99.
14. Acts 17:27–28
15. John 14:17, 20
16. Bourgeault, *Mystical Hope,* 31.
17. Linn et al., *Understanding,* 77.

the Western church, Rohr has become a major advocate for the nurture of the experience of immanence; based on Thomas Merton, he calls this experience True Self, the immortal diamond.[18] It sounds like Rohr would not be surprised by how baffled I was, nor would he regard my bafflement as foolish!

A second explanation that suggests a connection between a left-brain culture and a preference for transcendent theology comes from David Benner, a clinical psychologist and writer. He knows firsthand the religious culture that would ask the question "How could God possibly encourage you to be yourself?" He placed Thomas Merton's words as epigraph to his book, knowing they would puzzle many contemporary Christians: "There is only one problem on which all my existence, my peace, and my happiness depend: to discover myself in discovering God. If I find Him I will find myself and if I find my true self I will find Him."[19] He draws upon the words of John Calvin, specifically recognizing that they might surprise the evangelical mind-set: "There is no deep knowing of God without a deep knowing of self and no deep knowing of self without a deep knowing of God."[20]

Benner suggests that Merton's insight is so jarring because it had fallen neglected in contemporary Christian spirituality, through our left-brain fixation with thoughts, which gained momentum in the Enlightenment: "Trust in God was slowly degraded . . . into trust in certain thoughts about God. . . . Thoughts are, quite simply, a poor substitute for relationship."[21] I have long concluded that all doctrine about God (ideas about God) must have originally started in some kind of lived experience[22], but we tend to get fascinated with our ideas, and when those ideas are not continually fed and interpreted by ongoing experience, they can become dead—and deadly. When religion becomes mostly about holding correct belief about

18. Rohr, *Immortal Diamond*. A few days after I thought I had completed this manuscript, I started reading *Immortal Diamond* and thus felt the need to add this footnote. I was stunned by the number of words and images he uses that are identical to those I had already been led to. He says "an unexplainable goodness is at work in the universe" (page xx). He describes us as the pearl of great price (118) and addresses the precise question I pose in the Prologue: "How can knowing ourselves help us know God?" (page 93). Reading *Immortal Diamond* felt like another pearl, another affirmation that what I have experienced is part of a much larger truth.

19. Merton, quoted in Benner, *Gift of Being Yourself*, 3.

20. Calvin, *Institutes*, 15.

21. Benner, *Soulful Spirituality*, 6.

22. I was pleased to discover that Aquinas says this! *Summa Theologica*, "De Anima," II,37: "*Prius vita quam doctrina ('Life is prior to doctrines').*" *Immortal Diamond*, xxv.

God (note the long statements of belief that many evangelical churches require of members), we become less and less open and willing, or trained, to encounter the living God, who might not only shake up our beliefs, but also transform us, from the inside, which is always more risky than playing with ideas. Maybe the Western focus on ideas about God has undermined our ability to trust in our experience, because don't experiences of the living God defy explanation? That's why the Bible is full of stories, and Jesus uses parables rather than making creedal statements. True experience of God is simply not predictable and containable. If we were taught to seek and expect and long for this kind of encounter, we would come to know what Richard Rohr calls "incarnational mysticism."[23] We would expect God's presence in our bodies, in our hearts, in our minds. We would not be left, as I was, stranded with an experience I felt I needed to justify theologically. Maybe it is only when our life experience challenges those beliefs (through grief or trauma or the messiness of life) and our sense of self is forced to expand to include more than our thoughts that we stand a chance of being drawn into deeper engagement with the *other*.

Whereas Underhill and Benner gave me intellectual ways to understand my experience, it was Lytta Basset's exploration of the biblical character Jacob that drew out of me a deep "Ah! That's it! She would understand what I experienced! She would not be surprised!" She traces Jacob's journey from Jacob-heel (who by disguise stole his brother's blessing) to Jacob the confronter, profoundly culminating in the mysterious wrestling at the Jabbok River, where he both realizes the promised blessing of God and discovers his own strength. They are intertwined. He has been living a dysfunctional life, caught up in the lies inherited from his family. But there is more to him. His pattern of fleeing and deception is not the deepest truth about him. At a certain point, he begins to affirm himself, which means standing up to his uncle Laban. "Why do some people begin to affirm themselves while others remain Jacob-heels all their lives? It seems to me it is a question of hearing. . . . For Jacob, it was the day when he heard the OTHER say to him, 'I want you to return to your country; I believe you can do it.'"[24] Basset translates this more universally to how God might speak to each of us: "I need you to be yourself; I need you to take your place."[25] Jacob's desire has been, all along, a desire planted in him by God:

23. Rohr, *Falling Upward*, 78.

24. Basset, *Holy Anger*, 143.

25. Ibid., 143.

"To be chosen is to want to be chosen. . . . The better we understand human desire, the more the priority of God is rendered invisible, *as is proper*. . . . God himself gives humans the desire that he wants to fulfill. For where did Jacob get this desire?"[26] The picture is of a God who wants Jacob to realize his own strength, his self, as God-given, God-blessed, God-celebrated. Basset concludes, "What lets us see that God is God? We can see this in the metamorphosis of a person who, one day, . . . finds himself or herself to be inhabited by a powerful Presence and takes his or her place among others. . . . The road travelled is one of incarnation."[27] There's that word again: incarnation. God and flesh united.

I suspect that, in a true encounter with God, we are drawn deeper into the experience of both transcendence and imminence: we take off our shoes in awe, we feel intimately spoken to, very aware that we are in the presence of *other,* and we also feel we ourselves have become more. Because this *other* is loving and creative, these encounters do not just astound us, but create us. After the wrestling at the Jabbok, Jacob says, "I have seen God face to face,"[28] and he is also ready to face the possibility of death, the risky encounter with another in the person of his brother, Esau, coming toward him with four hundred men.

It is the voice at the Jabbok, which knows him (touches him at the most deep level, at his deepest wound, represented by his thigh) and names him, that transforms Jacob's earlier raw "I am afraid!"[29] The voice is always pushing at the walls of our bondage, at whatever separates us, one from another and us from our true selves. Upon reading Basset's account of the encounter at the Jabbok, I wondered whether the question that I heard, "What would you need?," was some version of the question that was posed to Jacob, "What is your name?," and the subsequent invitation to know and celebrate his true self. I also began to wonder whether every encounter with the *other* is a kind of renaming, like Jacob experienced. If Lectio Divina is an encounter that changes us irrevocably, then maybe we are always being renamed to live into our identity ever more deeply.

I suspect that although there are various explanations for the power of the detractor accusation ("It's all about you!") in the history of Western thought, maybe the real root of it lies in the incredibility of the gospel:

26. P. Beauchamp in Basset, *Holy Anger,* 140.

27. Basset, *Holy Anger,* 153.

28. Gen 32:30

29. Gen 32:11

God so loves the world[30]. How can God do this? Why would God, who is Spirit, love the world? Maybe in their deepest hearts, human beings do not like themselves and can't believe God can. Or maybe we sense the risk involved in living as if God were inside us: it radically changes how we treat ourselves and others. Newness emerges when we begin to trust that spirit and flesh can mingle, and do, as shown in the person of Jesus. The invitation is to trust that they mingle in us too. The invitation is to trust that as we venture into this newness, and inevitably stumble, we will nevertheless, and always, be held in love.

The talk about selfhood is challenging. People experienced in contemplative prayer say that in the end, we realize that what we thought was ourself is stripped away, and that this stripping is a very crucial step in discovering our True Self. I answered the voice's question with a list of four characteristics of the person Cathy that I recognized. Maybe those four characteristics are not the deepest truth about Cathy. Maybe someday even those qualities I hold dear will be stripped away in the face of a challenge or a suffering that drives me to my knees. But maybe in the process of helping me see what looked like solid ground (what compassion!), the voice simultaneously revealed the only solid ground there is for human beings: our capacity to recognize, trust, and love the voice. That is our truest, deepest self.

This brings us to a significant question. Was this voice only for me or does it carry a graceful message to others as well? Would the telling of this story lead others deeper into love of themselves and others? If the message, and this experience, is only for me, then this is simply an interesting story. But if the message tells us something about that *other* whose essence is love, then maybe this is a kind of epiphany that needs to be shared. Is the *other* saying the same thing to anyone who will listen? If so, I am likely not the only one to receive it. There should be others hearing that same voice giving them permission to seek and trust in their True Self, because their *I* is not completely separate from the *other*. This is the point of Richard Rohr's description of the second half of life, once we have been pushed out of the first half by the painful messiness of life and surrendered to the voice that calls after the True Self.[31]

I conclude that the question with which I wrestled is a very good one, leading to the heart of the gospel. The either/or nature of it, forcing me to

---

30. John 3:16
31. Rohr, *Falling Upward*, 92.

see the voice as either of God or not, reveals the limitation of our minds, which operate in dualisms. In trusting the voice, I was not simply trusting in myself. I was trusting in both *other* and, through the voice, because of the voice, myself. It was like being given a new name, as is promised in Isaiah 62:4: "You shall no more be termed Forsaken, and your land shall no more be termed Desolate; but you shall be called My Delight Is in Her." This story of mine seems to be about trusting in and surrendering to the voice that communicates delight.

One sunny Sunday afternoon, a group of women, all from conservative evangelical backgrounds, sat around in my living room, discussing a book we had read together. One woman blurted out, "I was taught not to trust in myself." There was an instant collective sigh heard around the room. I was astonished by the clarity of the sigh: we all knew it, in our very bones.

So, it is not just me who needs this message. This voice is good news for many. It is good news for women in a patriarchal culture. It is good news for Christians in the Western church that has emphasized mostly transcendence and correct belief, not training us to interpret or even recognize our experience. It is good news for all of us taught to turn to experts and their logic, ignoring the wisdom our bodies know. Our selves get lost.

Maybe this is the good news: the One who said, "Ah! This is so very good!" is still saying it. And when we are led to hear it, we are transformed in the direction of the goodness, which includes all we are. And it is not sin to be who we are.

I am sure the transcendents throw up all kinds of warning flags at this point. I know the warnings well: we human beings have a penchant toward self-deception. We choose only what we want to hear; we choose what makes us comfortable. If this is so, though, where is the power of God to break through our deceptions and set us free? If we trust more in our deceivability than in God's power to speak lovingly, what has become our god?

When I finally did see Sister Meg, on the last day of the retreat, she affirmed what I had discovered: *the voice* knew me. She advised about the necessary distinction between trusting in myself and trusting in *the voice*. They are distinct. I am not *the voice*. But *the voice* does speak; *the voice* dwells within, and *the voice* loves us in all our glorious incompleteness.

16

LOOKING FOR THE IRREVOCABLE

The ability to inhabit the darkness patiently and not despair, but, by learning to tell a new story . . . to help ourselves and others reimagine a goodness that we never thought was available to us, is not the least of what the Spirit makes possible.

JAMES ALISON, *FAITH BEYOND RESENTMENT*[1]

Nineteen months post-surgery, someone asked me, "What has been the upshot of all this for you?" The "all this" gave me lots of latitude: What is the upshot of having a tumor removed from my head? What is the upshot of losing an ear but keeping my face? What is the upshot of hearing a voice that knows me? What is the upshot of receiving an answer to a lifelong prayer? What is the upshot of being given what I had called "the most precious thing in all the world"? What is the upshot of an encounter that is said to change a person irrevocably, moving us from "light to light of wisdom and heart to heart of compassion"?[2]

---

1. Alison, *Faith Beyond Resentment*, 167.
2. Funk, "Sustained Lectio Divina."

I have decided to answer all of the above. I approach the question slowly, in true Lectio fashion, starting with the most obvious, visible changes that can be seen and felt and measured.

To a casual observer, and even to one who studies my face carefully, my medical history is not evident. There is no visible sign of what I have been through. The scar on my head is hidden under my hair, and the scar on my belly would only be noticed if I wore a bikini, which I don't. It has been fun to try to watch medical residents puzzle over the belly scar: it is not the usual location for any typical surgery. The physical requirements of my vocation, a tongue and mouth that make shapes so people can understand the sounds they produce, have been mostly unaffected. My eye blinks as it always has. My tongue is prompted on both sides by an intact facial nerve. This lack of visible change can make the adventure seem almost surreal.

But I am not the same. I hear nothing in my right ear. I have to be much more intentional about my personal geography and how I place my body in relation to others, more crucial the closer people get. Circles and semicircles, supposedly socially friendly geometries, are the most challenging. Rectangles are easier: if I place myself in either the southeast or northwest corner, I can hear almost everyone. Straight lines are even better: everyone on my left. But lines are hard to come by. If I can maneuver things, I put the louder-voiced people on my right so their voices will more easily carry around the obstacle now posed by my head and into my left ear. I do not and cannot engineer every social situation. I miss parts of conversations, and there have been more than a few unsuspecting victims who consider me either rude or spacey: I appear to be ignoring them or very distracted. A waitress who approaches me on my right side, outside my peripheral vision, goes unnoticed. That's a casualty I work with, unless I want an apparatus in my right ear that will transmit a voice into an apparatus in my left ear and thus into my head, to register itself. Unaccustomed to wearing apparatus of any kind, I am loath to investigate this option.[3] Does this mean I prefer to experience deafness and some social awkwardness? I wish I could sport some kind of weightless, hologram message that floated quietly beside my head alerting all strangers: "This ear does not work!"

The complete lack of sensation on the right half of my head continues, with sporadic interjections of abnormal sensation. A cold wind or stress

3. Since writing this, I have invested in this two-part system, which makes use of Bluetooth technology. I wear it some; it works well in small groups and quieter rooms. Nothing really helps in a loud noisy room, and I do get impatient with the added fiddliness of it.

or strong emotion creates a predictable sense of tightness on one half of my face. That tightness can be very distracting and sometimes disabling: I become self-conscious about trying to make my smile symmetrical. Occasionally and with no discernible pattern I get a shooting pain right to the tip of my nose, so excruciating that it grinds conversation to a halt. I do not want to imagine what it would be like if the trigeminal nerve got seriously riled up.

Because I have no sensation in my right eye, it is vulnerable in some obvious and some not so obvious ways. I wear eye protection when I am out in the forest because I would not feel a branch brushing up against that side of my face or poking into my eye. One day some laundry detergent splashed up into my left eye, stinging so badly that I needed to flush it out. I realized I had no idea whether it went into my right eye as well, so I flushed it too. But I was perturbed to realize that if it hadn't splashed into my left eye, I wouldn't have known there might be something in my right.

After I shampoo in the shower, my right eye is always red and my left not. Does that mean shampoo has dribbled into it? How? I don't know. What does this all mean about ongoing incremental damage to my cornea? I check my eye in the mirror every day for redness because I would not have any other way to detect a foreign substance or an injury to it. My right eye contracts when I am tired. I can see the difference.

When I brush my teeth at night, I regularly find pieces of food that have been sitting there possibly for hours, unnoticed. A genteel eater I am not: pieces of food routinely end up hanging from the right corner of my mouth. In fancier social settings, I conscientiously remember to wipe that corner after every bite. More often than not, it is my eating companions who give me the subtle signal to remind me to wipe. I feel like a child or a nursing home resident. Red wine leaves a stain on the right side of my mouth, not my left. I could spend my life looking in the mirror. I am often mortified when I do. Or I laugh. Sometimes there is blood trickling down my cheek. The right side of my face is mosquito banquet ground for those lucky enough to chance upon it. I will not swat them away.

There are some upsides. I can intentionally bang one side of my head against a wall for the symbolic or kinetic satisfaction of the gesture but not feel the pain. I can accidentally bang that side of my head on a kitchen cabinet door and have no reason to swear. I can happily endure endless amounts of electrolysis to get rid of the gangly dark hairs on the right side of my chin; there is no pain threshold.

On the symbolic/metaphorical level, I am now a frayed and nibbled survivor in a fallen world: I have shifted from being a hardly hospitalized, hardly scarred, hardly even stitched up, all faculties working, pain-free person to being one who gimps through life. And I am getting along. While I have a number of idiosyncratic limitations to deal with, all of them are manageable. And I have lots of good company. Now, when I meet a person with some physical impairment, someone who can't move as fast as I would like them to, or who can't hear me, or when I come to a hospital bedside, I am attentive to any inner recoil within me. I push myself: that could be me; that is me! I will have less adjustment when I get to eighty and join the folks in the nursing home. I will have already been humbled some.

But I was also given other words with which to receive my frayed and nibbled-ness. Sometime before my surgery, I received a message from someone who had gone through some serious medical events of his own: *You are very privileged. I don't mean this in the sense that at most 20 percent of the world's population has access to the surgery you will receive—that is simply the privilege of context. You don't actually have to do anything with that privilege other than show up at the right time and place. I mean the privilege of being broken. . . . The breaking of a human life, of a human heart, is a profound gift. It opens us to others and opens others to us in ways that are not normally possible. But only to the extent that we allow the shattering to occur, only to the extent that we willingly relinquish our life and trust in a new life.*

This is another way to look at my life. I am the recipient of the privilege of being broken, to the extent that I allow the shattering to occur. Have I embraced the shattering?

It is not only all the physical changes that have affected me. What happened, I venture, was a shift in my center of gravity. I grew up very much a "head" person. Being smart was who I was. It still is: I like to understand. I analyze. When anxious, I overthink. But another strand grows. Maybe the strand began to take root twenty years earlier, when at age thirty-three I was thrown into the deep end: a ministry situation far over my head. No smart strategy worked. No strategy at all worked. I began to pray in a different way: empty-handed. I had to let go and trust in what I did not understand. The tumor decision felt like it deepened and thickened this strand, pushing it deeper into my being. The voice, after all, could not be explained. But it had real effect. This strand moves me out of my head and down into my heart.

I make decisions in different ways now. I still do the pros and cons and analyze. But then I also pay attention to how my heart responds to my head. When my logical capacities get stuck, I draw pictures—they reveal things my head can't touch. Looking at my artwork, my son thinks this is downright weird. In the end, what matters is not so much what I can understand but how I love. Can I call this a shift in identity? I am not sure that is up to me to name. I don't want to leap into a dichotomy between head and heart. I hope it is more like a weaving together, a stretching of who I am, a widening of my tent.

Paying attention to my life, in Lectio fashion, has led me to make some choices I never thought imaginable. Three years post-surgery found me living in an apartment in the city, going through a divorce, and unemployed. I'm sure it didn't look, to many an outside observer, like anything good, or anything to do with love. John O'Donohue's words, which had puzzled me at first, capture some of the complexity and impetus for this painful turning point: "You can never love another person unless you are equally involved in the beautiful but difficult spiritual work of learning to love yourself."[4] The movement that became so evident at the opera, learning to trust in who I am, learning to trust the "God in me," kept pushing me through sadness and forms of death.

I gather from Sister Meg that such momentous changes are not surprising: when people really start doing Lectio seriously, listening to the text of their lives, things start to change. Awareness leads to upheaval. Awareness can cost a lot. I feel as if I walk sometimes not knowing much at all, just tracking the fragrance of life, as best as I can.

I realize that the support I received through diagnosis and surgery, which in my case was mostly over the course of four months, would be more difficult for a community to sustain over a longer stretch (cancer, for instance) or for a circumstance more complex (divorce, for instance). While I am amazed and grateful for the community that gathered around me to support me through my surgery, I am also aware that communities have their limits. For most of the things we go through, it is a few good friends we need.

The third voice of a text (which Sister Meg calls the moral/dynamic) assumes that the text invites response, in both prayer and action. What do I do differently now? Is there a change in how I love my neighbor? I find myself taking risks (like writing this book!) and venturing things I never

4. O'Donohue, *Anam Cara*, 26.

would have before, like offering to work with groups suffering in conflict. I don't enjoy conflict. Few people do. It pushes all of our ego buttons and tests every ounce of faith and love. My ego's fear of criticism and failure holds me back; my trust in God for my identity pushes me forward despite my fear.

Do I pray more or differently now that I have had this very pointed response to my prayers? My prayer life wends its way, as eclectic as ever. I am aware that it might be a temptation to chase down another such experience—so clear and profound. That might be as futile as looking for the perfect medical solution about which my Toronto neurosurgeon warned me. On the other hand, Cynthia Bourgeault insists that encounters with God are not intended to be regarded as extraordinary, but "*an abiding state of being.*" It is our responsibility "to develop a conscious and permanent connection to this wellspring" called the Mercy through contemplative prayer.[5] After all, Jesus says to the woman at the well: "The water that I will give will become *in them* a spring of water gushing up to eternal life."[6] (italics mine) Do I find it any easier to do the silent listening of the mystical/contemplative practice? Sigh. No! I still have to exercise great discipline and trust. I still have to simply keep going to the silence, and waiting, and living with the not-knowing. I do not control the voice. I never know when I will get some kind of whiff of an answer to the question I am posing. I pose lots. I wait lots. I also find that God works with what we offer, in great mercy.

My spiritual director says that prayer is really about *stance*. I think she means humility, wonder, and openness. I think she means something like what Martin Buber says about leaders in the Bible. Their most important quality is that they stay in the dialogue.[7] I stay in the dialogue. I do not expect another so clear voice, but I do keep asking the questions, about everything. I keep looking for signs in the day-to-day events of my life for the One I believe lives in this world, elusively but beautifully. It is hugely comforting to remember the kind gentleness of that question: "What would you need?" I try to let that kindness continue to shape me. As I do, hopefully it will shape some irrevocable changes.

How do I act?

I think I have learned something profound about the need to not-do and the place of not-trying. I used to be a one-mode person: try try try; work work work. It is quite different to have some kind of partnership

5. Bourgeault, *Mystical Hope*, 17.

6. John 4:15

7. Buber, *On the Bible*, 148.

between working hard and doing nothing. It is a practice not unlike the listening part of Lectio Divina. Sometimes we have to shut up, let our hands drop to our sides, still our minds, and just listen. It is amazing what can happen. "It is not by dint of labour," St. Teresa says about the mystic's way.[8] Rather, grace comes when we are able to receive. Grace comes when our hands have been emptied.

Carol's question, "Why don't you stop trying?," comes laden with gifts for a culture that idolizes the type A personality. One is the gift of play (nondirective, nonproductive, pleasurable activity). Researchers are finding that people who play end up being better workers. I know I will receive many gifts of play from my grandchildren! Other gifts are silence and rest, and relinquishing our self-sufficiency. In relinquishing self-sufficiency we develop a capacity to receive from others. We take our place in the web.

The question I was asked at the opera, "What would you need?," sounds like the question Benedictines always ask of their guests: "What do you need?" It is a question of hospitality, and it reminds me of George Herbert's poem "Love," where the voice is "sweetly questioning / If I lack'd anything." There can be no grace if we cannot create space to receive. That space is created by subtracting, by intentionally taking away. Our culture does not teach us how to take away. We only learn how to add, surrounding ourselves with more and more. To create space, not knowing what will fill the emptiness, is profoundly countercultural. It takes a spiritual practice to do nothing, to wait, to listen, to fall silent.

Trust in who I am continues to be something into which I grow. Psychologist David Benner's words have encouraged me to pay attention and trust at several critical junctures.[9] Like Parker J. Palmer (*Let Your Life Speak*) and Thomas Merton, talking about the true and false self, Benner knows my enemy: a religious stance that tells me what I should be rather than accepting who I am. Both Benner and Palmer recount the same Hasidic story. Rabbi Zusya said, "I have learned that God will not ask me, 'Why were you not Moses, leading your people out of slavery?' Nor will he ask me, 'Why were you not Joshua, leading your people into the Promised Land?' God will say to me, 'Zusya, there was only one thing that no power of heaven or earth could have prevented you from becoming. Why were you not Zusya?'" The voice at the opera pushed me in this same direction,

---

8. Underhill, *Mysticism,* 64.

9. Benner, *Gift of Being Myself* and *Soulful Spirituality.*

essentially asking, "Who are you?" I continue to have to pay attention and honor and trust in who I am.

On the fourth level of *Lectio Divina*, I am supposed to simply wait and do nothing, simply receive. Now is the time to tell how I arrived at the title for this book. Years ago our family had a series of uncanny coincidences that even Ted had to say felt like Providence. We ended up renting a house in southern France that met our desires far beyond anything we could have maneuvered by clever research. When we went to visit, out of curiosity, the house we had almost rented in a village in the Alsace, our mouths gaped: the town was in the middle of a year-long construction project that had jackhammers at work right outside the door where we would have lived. Ted, with his deep need for quiet, could not refrain from the language of his childhood: "I have been saved!"

Later we mused that this language of Providence was very perturbing: "But we don't believe in Providence!" At least, not in the way we had somehow picked up in evangelical circles: "God has a beautiful plan for your life, and you can just watch it unfold." But we had been given a goodness that was so gracious, so extravagant, and so apparently tailored to our deepest desires. We could not explain it. When I recounted this to a Presbyterian mentor friend, he exclaimed, "It's a second naïveté!," referring to the work of philosopher Paul Ricoeur. In our second naïveté, we embrace again words and ideas from our childhood that our critical reasoning has led us to abandon. Through the force of life experience, we pick them up again, but in a new way, with different, renewed meaning. Life pushes us to wonder again; life ushers us into awe.

This experience in France became for me a diamond I could forever carry around in my pocket, unwrap, and ponder when in need. I could call it to mind the way those Hebrews called to mind their exodus from Egypt. So, sometime after returning from France, I was working in the church. The doorbell rang. Two seventeen-year-old young men from the local high school stood there. Sheepishly they explained that they had a philosophy assignment due the next day: could they interview me about my belief in God? How could I say no to that? I gave up the plan of getting home on time at the end of a long day and led them up to the sanctuary. Pushing a microphone up to my mouth they asked, "Why do you believe in God?"

I laughed and said, "Because of all the goodness I cannot explain." Don't ask me where my words came from. I hadn't planned this response. I hadn't calculated or reasoned it. The words just descended as if from the sky, or leapt up as if from an underground spring. They appeared and I received them. That is a form of the fourth, contemplative sense: one simply receives. One can't count on such moments. One simply recognizes them. The more I mused over what had come out of my mouth, the more I liked it. It posed an edgy challenge to the run-of-the-mill too-easy cynicism that records only the evil in the world.

But those words call me to account as well. What is the goodness that I refer to? At first, maybe it was a house in the woods in France, away from the sound of jackhammers. Then maybe it became a string of kind people, appearing in my life at just the time I needed them. But if it all just stopped there, then what happens when circumstances change? When I end up living with a jackhammer? When the tumor is not benign? When I don't have a choice in doctors? when there is no doctor?

New Testament scholar Eduard Schweizer has been a profound teacher:

> An event is a miracle only if God speaks to us in it. . . . Occasionally God has to wave a flag before our faces, so to speak, in order to make us sit up and take notice. . . . In the act of healing itself nothing important has happened unless there is a personal encounter with Jesus. . . . Faith comes to fulfillment only in a personal encounter with Jesus, in dialogue with him. Without this there is no value in the experience of miracles which stagger the imagination.[10]

Miracles, Schweizer says, have to do with the birth of faith: the believer learns of God's acceptance of us into a relationship that death will not terminate. The real miracle of the resurrection is the emergence of faith that believes God is able to triumph over death, that on the day of our death, we are able to trust we are held in love, even as our bodies fall into decay.[11]

To try to extrapolate from my teacher: all the goodness I received, all those pearls I felt were strung around my neck, all those kind actions toward me, mean little if they do not lead me to actions of trust, actions that are qualitatively different because they arise from trusting that my life and my death, my body, and everything I can see and do, is held in love. The ups

10. Schweizer, *Good News*, 108, 117–18, 120.

11. Ibid., 121.

and downs of life's circumstances, tumors malignant and benign, doctors kind and brusque, they are all held.

I have been the recipient of many goodnesses I cannot explain, goodnesses that stagger my imagination. I could say that I hope it means I am "becoming a pearl," like when my mother said to me when I was a teenager, going away on some adventure, "May you become a blessing," which struck me as very strange at the time. We say blessings; we don't *become* them (so I thought). It would sound far too straightforward to say, "I hope I will become an unexplainable good to the people around me." I have no confidence that I can do and be that goodness. But I hope I can. I hope that thankfulness works something in me, which can be seen. I don't know how that comes about.

When I first answered that question, "Why do you believe in God?," and spoke of goodness, I think it was all the little pearls of my life that had caught my attention, their little flags waving. They were the goodness. They astonished me. They led me to a second naïveté, an openness to some kind of refiguring of Providence. They led me back to a sense of wonder that is not pre-logic like a child's, but comes post-logic, or "along with logic," or "despite the usual logic." The goodness has now taken a different shape. Patiently knitting together all that is, Mercy herself is the goodness I cannot explain.

ACKNOWLEDGMENTS

T he story in this book does not belong to me. It arises from a web of graceful encounters with the people described on these pages: an emergency doctor, a few neurosurgeons, an otolaryngologist, more than one physiotherapist, and a host of friends, neighbors, family. Many of them need to remain anonymous, for various reasons; some have their names changed. My friend Carol Wood asked the pivotal question. My spiritual director Sister Mary did and still does ask many questions I cannot answer. Sister Meg Funk opened doors I didn't know existed. Without them, there would be no story to tell.

There were those who mostly suffered along beside me. At times I know they felt even more helpless than I did. To my children, parents, and family, the congregation of St. Cuthbert's, the Women touched by Grace, and one in particular who suffered in ways I will never know: thank you for your prayers and your words and your willingness to walk alongside. You were my coracle.

A writers' workshop, *Believing in Writing*, at Collegeville Institute for Ecumenical and Cultural Research, led by Michael Dennis Browne, helped me believe I could write this. I am indebted to the Institute for funding that workshop and to that group of twelve, particularly Marjorie Stelmach, and Mary O'Connor who read through an initial draft with great care.

John Terpstra, Dr. Andrea Frolic, Dr. Gerald Janzen, Dr. Vicky Chen, Michael Pennanen, and Colleen Vanderelst graciously read through the manuscript and offered helpful insights and suggestions. Maggi Jamieson (MSW) read it through more than once. Her experiences working in the ICU ward and our conversations about suffering and death helped crystallize why I was writing this story and to whom it might speak. My sister Elizabeth cheered me on and gave publishing advice. I am deeply moved to be able to grace the cover of this book with Erica Grimm's artwork. I cannot imagine a more fitting image. My daughter Sarah (now a Doctor of Theology) talked with me about John Calvin. Alison Gresik reentered my life like one of those stunning gifts that cannot be explained. She offered not only copyediting skill but also loving queries that clarified and sharpened everything. She became the editor I didn't know I needed. Ralph Vyn helped me think through the prologue and patiently supported me through many a long Saturday afternoon devoted to "the book." There were those who pestered and waited patiently in expectation, believing this was a story needing to be told. They pulled this writing out of me. There were those who, upon hearing what happened at the opera, told me their spines tingled. That assured me of the beauty of this story. There were others who asked difficult questions, and this manuscript is more honest and loving because of them.

This story may have been written, but not sent out into the world, if it weren't for Rowan Williams' words in *Resurrection,* about the web of gift exchange that binds the church together through the exchange of stories and memories: "'Love your neighbour as yourself': love in the mode that emerges from the past that is yours and no one else's, out of the process in which you have learned to accept yourself. Begin to see your self as gift, love it as gift, from God's hand."[1]

---

1. Williams, *Resurrection*, 44.

Appendix A

CRANIAL NERVES

Cranial Nerve	Major Functions
I Olfactory	Smell
II Optic	Vision
III Oculomotor	Motor: Eyelid and eyeball movement; pupil constriction
IV Trochlear	Motor: Turns eye downward and some lateral
V Trigeminal	Motor: Chewing Sensory for face, nose, tongue, teeth.
VI Abducens	Turns eye laterally (away from nose)
VII Facial	Controls most facial expressions Secretion of tears and saliva Taste from front of tongue
VIII Vestibulocochlear (auditory)	Hearing Equilibrium sensation

IX Glossopharyngeal	Taste from back of tongue; some swallowing; Some sensations Senses carotid blood pressure
X Vagus	Senses aortic blood pressure Slows heart rate Stimulates digestive organs Taste
XI Spinal Accessory	Controls muscles used in head movements Controls swallowing movements
XII Hypoglossal	Controls tongue movements

Appendix B

My Medical Summary
of the Two Options

March 2007
Two possible (equally good) treatment paths for Cathy's vestibular schwannoma (VS)

NOTE: This was the medical information I was given in 2007, to the best of my memory and notes from that time. In most details it is very similar, but does not completely match, the information currently put out by the Acoustic Neuroma Association in the US. This summary, therefore, should not be taken as a final word for medical advice, but does illustrate the complexity of this kind of medical decision.

On two questions, the variance is more significant. Years post-surgery, I was told by the CEO of the Acoustic Neuroma Association of the US that I would not have been offered radiation in the US given the size of my tumor. Had I lived in the US, then, I might not have this story to tell: an interesting circumstance to ponder. I cannot comment on the medical reasons for the differences between the advice their association has been given and the advice I was given. I did, however, think it important to acknowledge this difference for readers whose interest in the medical details is crucial. The CEO also said that they had been advised that the risk of malignancy from radiation was not as high as 1 percent: it was "rare." This also would have impacted my story, perhaps. This alternative information, given post-surgery, does not take away what I regard as the heart of this story.

SURGERY

Goal: remove tumor completely
Chance of complete removal: 98 percent
Chance of morbidity (death on operating table): I think he said 0.5 percent

Losses

Hearing

Complete and definitive loss of hearing in right ear, because the method of entry destroys the bones of the ear (this is the only possible way of entry, because of size and position of tumor)

Facial Nerve

20 percent chance of permanent damage to the facial nerve.

Permanent damage means: eye does not close (drying out is a big risk; would need to be covered at night and irrigated manually); facial droop; asymmetrical smile (can't lift that side of the mouth); possible drool; possible speech problems (not clear on this; surgeon didn't talk about it, but some of the literature does).

There will certainly be some temporary damage, so whether the damage is permanent wouldn't be known for three to four months or even a year.

If there is permanent damage, these are the possible corrective procedures:

- Plastic surgery to correct the droop

- Nerve graft from the tongue to the eye, to help eye close, but then tongue would have to work from one nerve (physiotherapy and speech therapy needed to adjust)

- No real hope for the smile, it seems, if the damage is permanent

Possible Complication

Spinal fluid leak. This does not weigh heavily on me, as it is a small chance.

Short-Term Challenge

The vestibular nerve would also be completely destroyed, and the nerve on the other side of the body needs to take over. I met a teacher who had a small (2 cm) tumor removed, and he said the regaining of balance took him much longer than the six weeks predicted. It had taken months, and his balance never recovered completely. He couldn't look up to catch a ball without losing his orientation, and doing the front crawl (always turning his head) was disorienting.

Medical Procedure

This is the most common method re VS, having been used for years, now enhanced by monitoring the nerve signals in the midst of the surgery.

The experience of the surgeon is the single most important factor in saving facial nerve.

Invasion of the skull always carries risks and consequences (headaches, fatigue for a while).

What My Life Might Look Like

This Spring

Surgery late April; six weeks of recuperation, physiotherapy for face and balance; but based on an account of a much smaller VS being removed, I'm guessing *at least* three months; three to four months of "wait and see" re damage to facial nerve.

Next Two Years

It all depends on damage to facial nerve.

If no permanent damage, probably some physiotherapy re partial damage, then life as usual, except for hearing loss.

If damage, then possibly slow regeneration and/or procedures and physiotherapy and adjustments re eye, tongue, facial muscles.

Long-term Future

Adjust to hearing loss; adjust to facial loss.

RADIATION

Goal: arrest growth of tumor
Control Rate: 90 to 95 percent chance of success
Chance of morbidity: 1 percent chance of inducing a malignancy over the next five to ten years; could be skin or brain tissue (any tissue affected by radiation). Malignancy does not mean death, but a malignant brain tumor is a wholly different ball game.

Losses

Hearing

70 percent chance of retaining current hearing ability, at least in the short term. There would be damage to the nerve, which would mean that hearing ability would decline with age at a faster rate than if not radiated.

Facial Nerve

2 to 3 percent chance of some damage/weakness

Possible Complications

Swelling: radiated tumors can swell as the cells die and release their fluids. If my tumor swells, it would press into cerebellum and brainstem, but the radiologist says there is room for swelling, given the position of my tumor. My tumor presses a little against the brainstem, but not much, not interfering with the signals going up and down it, and the stem can accommodate more pressure. This sounds a little scary, as the brainstem controls all major functions: breathing, heart, etc.

Hydrocephalous: 5 percent chance of developing hydrocephalous, which would be treated with installing a shunt. (where would the shunt be?)

If tumor does not die, then surgery would be needed. It would take about two years to tell whether the tumor has died or not. About two-thirds of tumors shrink; one-third simply remain the same size, but are arrested.

Medical Procedure

Fractionated Stereotactic Radiotherapy given at the Pencer Brain Tumor Centre at Princess Margaret Hospital in Toronto.

Twenty-five radiation sessions, at 200 rads each, for a total of 5000 rads or 50 Gy. Contra the literature, this is NOT a relatively new way to treat VS. It's only the stereotactic part that is new, which means more accuracy. It was developed in response to patients (and doctors, I presume) wanting a less invasive method, with less damage to facial nerve and hearing. Radiologist says there are reports of the use of radiotherapy for large acoustic neuromas with fifteen to thirty years follow-up using fractionated radiotherapy. The newer technique of stereotactic fractionated radiation is just more accurate, but same radiotherapy doses. The 1 percent risk of malignancy is based on thousands of patients with benign brain tumors undergoing radiotherapy in the same area. For every acoustic they treat, they treat a few hundred other types of brain tumors.

Recent technology has allowed a way to ensure the exact repositioning of the head each day. They now have improved that and, with the help of a daily CT scan, can pinpoint the tumor each day with excellent precision.

When we asked the radiologist which of the two treatment paths he would choose for himself, or for his wife, he said it was 50/50. His two biggest concerns re the radiation are (1) the 1 percent risk of malignancy and (2) the swelling.

This Pencer Brain Tumor Centre is the best in Canada, and people come from around the world to learn from them. It is devoted to brain tumors, though they have not treated many VS tumors my size. They have treated many smaller ones. Mine is unusual to be this size (usually too big for radiation) and yet positioned so as not pressing overly on brainstem (as in, there remains room for it to swell).

This method, as it does not remove the tumor, would require monitoring, to see if tumor dies, changes, or shrinks.

What My Life Might Look Like

This Spring

Treatment could start within ten days of my decision, so late March, possibly, through April, with daily commuting to Toronto. I would be off work. Hard to say if recuperation time would be needed following radiation, as everyone is different. Some say I might need another five to six weeks to recover from fatigue.

Swelling, if it occurs, is in the three to nine months following treatment (as cells expire), so three to nine months of waiting/watching.

Current symptoms might continue or might cease. They often cease, even without shrinkage of tumor. I have "soft" symptoms, and they are tolerable, though I don't know what it would be like to have them for the rest of my life! I think it would be OK.

Next Two Years

Current symptoms might continue or might cease
Monitoring tumor size/change (a few MRIs, I'm guessing)
Watching for symptoms caused by swelling and/or hydrocephalous

Long-term Future

Slow deterioration of hearing
Living with the 1 percent malignancy risk
Possible continuation of current symptoms

THE MAIN DIFFERENCES

Surgery involves *immediate and obvious, visible, "mechanical" physical loss,* and then slow rehabilitation.

In the short term (three to nine months post-treatment) radiation might involve some procedures, stronger symptoms, but *likely no immediate change, for good or for ill.* Rather, there is the long-term risk to live with, and the waiting to see if the treatment worked.

Radiologist said that if I were twenty-nine, they would not consider radiation; surgery would be the medical choice. At age sixty-nine, they'd probably recommend radiation. Me being age forty-nine, I'm in the middle: not clear which is best. I'm not clear what the significance of age is, actually.

BIBLIOGRAPHY

Alison, James. *Faith Beyond Resentment: Fragments Catholic and Gay.* New York: Crossroad, 2001.

——. *The Joy of Being Wrong: Original Sin Through Easter Eyes.* New York: Crossroad, 1998.

Angier, Natalie. *The Canon: A Whirligig Tour of the Beautiful Basics of Science.* New York: Houghton Mifflin, 2007.

Basset, Lytta. *Holy Anger: Jacob, Job, Jesus.* Grand Rapids, MI: Eerdmans, 2007.

Benner, David. *The Gift of Being Yourself: The Sacred Call to Self-Discovery.* Downer's Grove, IL: InterVarsity Press, 2004.

——. *Soulful Spirituality: Becoming Fully Alive and Deeply Human.* Grand Rapids, MI: Brazos Press, 2011.

Berry, Wendell. *A Place on Earth.* 1967. Revised reprint, Washington, DC: Counterpoint, 2001.

——. "The Boundary." In *The Wild Birds.* Berkeley, CA: North Point Press, 1985.

Block, Peter. *Community: The Structure of Belonging.* San Francisco: Berrett-Koehler, 2009.

Bourgeault, Cynthia. *Mystical Hope: Trusting in the Mercy of God.* Lanham, MD: Cowley, 2001.

——. *The Wisdom Jesus: Transforming Heart and Mind—A New Perspective on Christ and His Message.* Boston: Shambhala, 2008.

Brown, Ian. "Doing the Work of the Heart." *Globe and Mail* (September 6, 2008). No pages. Online: http://www.theglobeandmail.com/news/national/doing-the-work-of-the-heart/article1060954.

Brueggemann, Walter. *Reverberations of Faith: A Theological Handbook of Old Testament Themes.* Louisville, KY: Westminster John Knox Press, 2002.

Buber, Martin. *On the Bible: Eighteen Studies.* Edited by Nahum N. Glazer. New York: Schocken Books, 1982.

Calvin, John. *Institutes of the Christian Religion.* 1536. Translated by Ford Lewis Battles. Grand Rapids, MI: Eerdmans, 1995.

de Chardin, Pierre Teilhard. "Patient Trust." In *Hearts on Fire: Praying with Jesuits,* 102–3. Edited by Michael Harter. 1993. Reprint, Chicago: Loyola Press, 2005.

Dillard, Annie. *Pilgrim at Tinker Creek*. 1974. Reprint, New York: Harper Perennial, 1998.

Funk, Mary Margaret. *Into the Depths: A Journey of Loss and Vocation*. New York: Lantern Books, 2011.

———. "Sustained Lectio Divina." Handout, 2007.

Gaskin, Ina May. *Ina May's Guide to Childbirth*. New York: Bantam Books, 2003.

Griswold, Frank T. "Listening with the Ear of the Heart." *CrossCurrents* (1998). No pages. Online: http://www.crosscurrents.org/griswold.htm.

Jones, Gregory L. *Embodying Forgiveness: A Theological Analysis*. Grand Rapids, MI: Eerdmans, 1995.

Leiner, Henrietta C. and Alan L. Leiner. "The Treasure at the Bottom of the Brain." *New Horizons for Learning* (September 1997). No pages. Online: http://education.jhu.edu/PD/newhorizons/Neurosciences/articles/The%20Treasure%20at%20the%20Bottom%20of%20the%20Brain/.

Linn, Matthew, et al. *Understanding Difficult Scriptures in a Healing Way*. New York: Paulist Press, 2001.

McEwan, Ian. *Saturday*. Toronto: Knopf Canada, 2005.

Major, Alice. "Eve waters the garden." In *Poetry as Liturgy: An Anthology by Canadian Poets*, edited by Margo Swiss, 65–68. Toronto: The St. Thomas Poetry Series, 2007.

Mukherjee, Siddhartha. *The Emperor of All Maladies: A Biography of Cancer*. New York: Scribner, 2010.

O'Donohue, John. *Anam Cara: A Book of Celtic Wisdom*. New York: Harper Perennial, 1998.

Oliver, Mary. *Thirst*. Boston: Beacon Press, 2006.

Palmer, Parker J. *Let Your Life Speak: Listening for the Voice of Vocation*. San Francisco: Jossey-Bass, 2000.

Roberts, Moss, trans. *Chinese Fairy Tales and Fantasies*. New York: Pantheon Books, 1979.

Rohr, Richard. *Falling Upward: A Spirituality for the Two Halves of Life*. San Francisco: Jossey-Bass, 2011.

———. *Immortal Diamond: The Search for Our True Self*. San Francisco: Jossey-Bass, 2013.

Severin, Tim. *The Brendan Voyage*. New York: McGraw-Hill, 1978.

Schweizer, Eduard. *The Good News According to Mark*. Translated by Donald H. Madvig. Atlanta: John Knox Press, 1970.

Stahl, Bill. *From the Beginning to the Exile*. The Bible's Story of Salvation 1. Bloomington, IN: iUniverse, 2008.

Taylor, Jill Bolte. *My Stroke of Insight: A Brain Scientist's Personal Journey*. New York: Viking, 2008.

Terpstra, John. *Skin Boat: Acts of Faith and other Navigations*. Wolfville: Gaspereau Press, 2009.

Trible, Phyllis. *God and the Rhetoric of Sexuality*. Philadelphia: Fortress Press, 1978.

Ueland, Brenda. *Strength to Your Sword Arm: Selected Writings*. Duluth, MN: Holy Cow! Press, 1996.

Underhill, Evelyn. *Mysticism: A Study in the Nature and Development of Man's Spiritual Consciousness*. New York: World Publishing, 1955.

Williams, Rowan. *Resurrection: Interpreting the Easter Gospel*. Harrisburg, PA: Morehouse, 1994.